thegoodwebguide

museums & galleries

www.thegoodwebguide.co.uk

thegoodwebguide

museums & galleries

matthew glanville

The Good Web Guide Limited • London

First Published in Great Britain in 2001 by The Good Web Guide Limited
Broadwall House, 21 Broadwall, London, SE1 9PL

www.thegoodwebguide.co.uk

Email:feedback@thegoodwebguide.co.uk

© 2001 The Good Web Guide Ltd

Text © 2001 Matthew Glanville

Original series concept by Steve Bailey.

Cover photo © Stone

10 9 8 7 6 5 4 3 2 1

A catalogue record for this book is available from the British Library.

ISBN 1-903282-14-4

Project Editor Michelle Clare

Design by Myriad Creative Ltd

Printed in Italy at LEGO S.p.A.

contents

the good web guides

The World Wide Web is a vast resource, with millions of sites on every conceivable subject. There are people who have made it their mission to surf the net: cyber-communities have grown, and people have formed relationships and even married on the net.

However, the reality for most people is that they don't have the time or inclination to surf the net for hours on end. Busy people want to use the internet for quick access to information. You don't have to spend hours on the internet looking for answers to your questions and you don't have to be an accomplished net surfer or cyber wizard to get the most out of the web. It can be a quick and useful resource if you are looking for specific information.

The Good Web Guides have been published with this in mind. To give you a head start in your search, our researchers have looked at hundreds of sites and what you will find in the Good Web Guides is a collection of reviews of the best we've found.

The Good Web Guide recommendation is impartial and all the sites have been visited several times. Reviews are focused on the website and what it sets out to do, rather than an endorsement of a company, or their product. A small but beautiful site run by a one-man band may be rated higher than an ambitious but flawed site run by a mighty organisation.

Relevance to the UK-based visitor is also given a high premium: tantalising as it is to read about purchases you can make in California, because of delivery charges, import duties and controls it may not be as useful as a local site.

Our reviewers considered a number of questions when reviewing the sites, such as: How quickly do the sites and individual pages download? Can you move around the site easily and get back to where you started, and do the links work? Is the information up to date and accurate? And is the site pleasing to the eye and easy to read? More importantly, we also asked whether the site has something distinctive to offer, whether it be entertainment, inspiration or pure information. On the basis of the answers to these questions sites are given ratings out of five. As we aim only to include sites that we feel are of serious interest, there are very few low-rated sites.

Bear in mind that the collection of reviews you see here are just a snapshot of the sites at a particular time. The process of choosing and writing about sites is rather like painting the Forth Bridge: as each section appears complete, new sites are launched and others are modified. When you've registered at the Good Web Guide site you can check out the reviews of new sites and updates of existing ones, or even have them emailed to you.

By registering at our site, you'll find hot links to all the sites listed, so you can just click and go without needing to type the addresses accurately into your browser.

All our sites have been reviewed by the author and research team, but we'd like to know what you think. Contact us via the website or email feedback@thegoodwebguide.co.uk. You are welcome to recommend sites, quibble about the ratings, point out changes and inaccuracies or suggest new features to assess.

You can find us at www.thegoodwebguide.co.uk

introduction

In putting together this book, we set out to ensure that our choices reflect the range and diversity of the museum experience. That's why anything from dinosaurs to ants, Sèvres, Lalique, conjoined twins, hermaphrodites, Pre-Raphaelites, post-modernists, Middle Kingdoms, heavy artillery and barns can all be found in the next 100 pages or so. The emphasis is almost entirely on those sites that are wholly – or at least have a high level – of English-language content. Consequently, the major museums of the United Kingdom and the USA predominate. However, there are some choices from around the world, with the exception of South America and the ice caps.

The internet has been scoured to come up with the hundred or so sites that you find reviewed here – scoured being the operative word. All the virtual museums and museum web directories that act as portals offer a tremendous number of options but little sense of quality. Those gathered here are genuinely the best of the web. Suggestions from friends and colleagues (often along the lines of 'I've seen a good museum in an obscure location and the curator was quite charming') have been followed up, however vague the recommendation might be. It is with this sense that 'we' is used throughout the reviews, since they represent a combined effort on the part of the author, kind friends and the publishers to track down sites all over the world. Despite this, the opinions expressed here, though often informed by first-hand knowledge, are no more impartial than anyone else's. If the reader spots certain common themes or perhaps idées fixes emerging through the reviews, then at least the author can't be charged with inconsistency.

The only certainty about the following reviews is their impermanence. Even during the writing, sites were being updated daily or even redesigned entirely. Online shops open and close as the institutions change their software. Links work and then fail because of server changes or an ill-considered redesign. Many would argue that this perpetual development makes the internet exciting and revolutionary, but it also makes any attempt to describe the success or otherwise of institutions' websites an ongoing project. Indeed, in conversation with a colleague at a major national museum recently, I discovered that they are not only planning an entirely new website for early next year – they are also planning the one that will replace that website in 18 months. With this in mind, please enjoy and use the following snapshots of museums and the internet, though be sure to check our website (www.thegoodwebguide.com) for the latest developments and innovations on the fastest growing media since the radio.

Matthew Glanville, June 2001

user key

£	Subscription
R	Registration Required
🔒	Secure Online Ordering

key to countries

AU	Austria	IT	Italy
AUS	Australia	JAP	Japan
CAN	Canada	KOR	Korea
D	Denmark	NL	Netherlands
FR	France	PO	Poland
G	Germany	RUS	Russia
		SP	Spain
		SW	Switzerland
		UK	United Kingdom
		US	United States

international heavyweights

Put simply, our first chapter is dedicated to size. While size doesn't always equal quality, these are the museums with international reputations and websites to match. Thematically, they tend to cover the decorative and fine arts simply because they tend to be the foci of large national galleries. Most of the collections were compiled in their present form in the 19th century, and they reflect the aggressive purchasing power and ambition of the European and North American museums and collectors of the period. Thanks to their foresight, and some might say vandalism, these museums have genuinely international collections and appeal.

The selection for this chapter largely reflects the international standing of the museums rather than a direct comment on their website. There are two notable exceptions. By any standards, the Vatican museum would rank among the finest museums in the world, but its website is frankly disappointing. Conversely, though famous among museum circles for its innovative displays and attention to detail, the American Museum of the Holocaust, while having a world-relevant theme, does not really have a world-renowned collection – however, it is included in this chapter because of the quality and depth of its site.

Unlike many of the other museums in this guide, those in this section have also been chosen with a view to their accessibility. There are museums in less well-known locations with comparable sites, but all those chosen for this chapter are in major tourist destinations; an alternative heading for this chapter might then be 'Ones you can visit easily'. Thus, more consideration has been given to the practical visitor aspects of the sites than is the case for some of the more geographically obscure sites reviewed. We make no apologies for this geographical chauvinism, because part of the use for any guide like this is to see what museums have on the website which reflects their collection. Many websites are in some sense tasters for the collection. You may be able to see and understand much of the collection through the web, but a true picture is only likely to emerge from a visit to the bricks-and-mortar site.

www.louvre.fr
Louvre Palace

Overall rating: ★ ★ ★ ★			
Classification:	Arts museum	Readability:	★ ★ ★ ★ ★
Updating:	Irregularly	Content:	★ ★ ★ ★ ★
Navigation:	★ ★ ★	Speed:	★ ★

FR 🔒

As one would expect from one of the major European collections, the feel of this site is one of sophistication and size. Like the museum, it wallows in the quality and scale of its collections, unfolding through pages which mirror in their size the rolling corridors of Europe's largest museum.

Browsers can choose between Spanish, Japanese, French and English language formats (though some areas are only in French) and the download of the initial text and pictures is quick. The left-hand side of the homepage offers a comprehensive choice of areas to explore, with sections on the history of the Louvre Palace and Museum, opening times, library facilities, and maps. Of particular interest to those planning to visit the Louvre is the option to purchase tickets online, along with an area describing which galleries can be guaranteed to be open at different times of the year. Having queued for what seemed like hours with vacant groups of Italian students in lines snaking round the Pyramide, the online ticket booking, with its special entrance and collection point, seems very opportune. The timetable of renovations should be compulsory on all large Museum sites, especially those in Italy where 'chiuso' often seems to be Italian for museum.

The collections are splendidly described. Explorations of the major works within the museum are broken down thematically so that, say, Classical Egypt is split into

have you registered for free updates?

log on to

www.thegoodwebguide.co.uk

sections on Religion and the Lower, Middle and Upper Kingdoms. These galleries are described in essays which illuminate the background to the galleries and the most notable items within the collection. To anyone not familiar with the Louvre collections, the scale and scope of these essays will come as a great pleasure.

Unsurprisingly, the Mona Lisa is the only individual item to receive a full treatment on its own – and this is only found in the online magazine. However, given the size and scope of the collections, their online treatment works well. The Online Magazine is full of information about the displays and forthcoming special exhibitions. The magazine is well thought-out and illustrated with in-depth articles, although some sections do not appear in translation.

SPECIAL FEATURES

Virtual Tour The link for this is on the homepage of the site, and is clearly an important and ambitious venture for the Louvre. The choice of galleries to explore is large, ranging from the Grand Empire to Ancient Egypt. Following the obligatory download of viewing software (QuickTime 4), which can take up to an hour to install (although many newer machines will have this installed already), the viewer can stand in a range of galleries, turning on the spot and zooming in and out to change the viewing angle. The number and range of these downloads is as vast as the museum itself, and they give a wonderful impression of the scope of the site. As ambitious as the Pyramid building that crowns the centre of the Louvre, these tours are a wonderful addition to what is already a comprehensive site. The download of the software may take a while but it is worthwhile, as it is used to great effect on many of the best museum websites we've reviewed. In combination with the wonderful gallery tours described above, these virtual tours almost make a visit to the Louvre unnecessary.

Online Shopping Featuring products almost entirely derived from the collection, the online shopping experience is both stylish and potentially expensive. All objects are illustrated and the range is good; for example, there are 49 posters available illustrated online. There is a currency converter to facilitate quotes in currencies, from the Finnish marka to the equally esoteric euro. The downsides are an overly compartmentalised catalogue and an unwieldy product search. These may make it easier to find specific items but it is difficult just to browse, and some shoppers may decide to give up rather than wait for the rather bizarre choices of the product finding service. This is, however, a small quibble when you take into account the wealth and quality of the range of products which dominate the online catalogue. The shop site operates an efficient online shopping service in which international buyers can have confidence.

The beauty and sophistication of the collections makes this site a wonderful experience.

www.metmuseum.org
Metropolitan Museum

Overall rating: ★ ★ ★ ★ ★			
Classification:	Arts museum	**Readability:**	★ ★ ★ ★
Updating:	Daily	**Content:**	★ ★ ★ ★ ★
Navigation:	★ ★ ★	**Speed:**	★ ★ ★ ★ ★

US 🔒

The Metropolitan Museum of Art's website reflects the Museum's status as an intellectual and artistic heavyweight at the top of any ranking of the world's museums. There is a changing piece of the day on the homepage reflecting the breadth and depth of the collection; recent examples have included rare Gauguin sketches and a sumptuous 15th-century Ethiopian Bible. While there is an attractive online shop with a vast range of objects (thousands), of greater interest is the online catalogue, with its images and text describing over 3,500 objects from the premier collections. This is no more than a reflection of the rigorous standards of the museum, but the site designers have had the courage to maintain these standards in the commentaries on each piece. In short, they don't insult their online audience. The quality of the images and the commentaries make this site compulsory for anyone who can't get to New York, whatever their historical or artistic interest.

The wealth of the collections and the quality of the visiting exhibitions is further underlined by the range of special exhibitions that have made their way onto the site. There are currently details of all the exhibitions held and to be held this year and next; from second-century BC Russia to 20th-century French painting, the range is fascinating. The depth of information provided about these exhibitions can be gauged from a brief survey of the content for the exhibition 'Painters in Paris 1895-1950'. One can follow links that give an overview of the exhibition, through images from it to sections that describe Cubism, Fauvism and other difficult modern art concepts. Cunningly there are links to educational packs, catalogues and posters from the online catalogue in the superb online store.

Much of this information can be emailed from the site to a friend, and they will also email you to remind you to go to the exhibition. The same amount of detail can be found for the other 15 or so special exhibitions, of which details appear on the site. Uniquely, the designers have taken care that much of this information is easily printable (you don't have to use the screen dump feature) and have also recognised that, with the printing of images in particular, different browsers and operating systems work in unique ways. To print at any stage, click on the printer icon and tick which printing system you are using; the results are much better than if you're using screen dumps. If you're unsure what system you are using, there are default options to make the whole process easier.

SPECIAL FEATURES

Gallery Complete a painless registration procedure (tick the box saying no mailings, it seems to work) and you can access this novel interactive facility. While some sites let you send a postcard in email form, here, using the wonderful images from the collections, you can create a virtual tour based on any theme or concept you choose. This is more fun than it sounds because it makes you wonder how to make someone else perceive the links you see between objects from any era or area of the collection. It is also a useful way of keeping your favourite objects readily accessible.

Online Shopping The Metropolitan boasts the largest museum bookstore in America, a boast reflected on their website with books on subjects as diverse as cuneiform and John Singer Sergent jostling for attention with ties, scarves and the like. There seem to be more books on the British Museum website but the Met's titles cover a wider range. The choice of goods is too wide to describe adequately and far larger than any other of the online museum's shops. Recognising this, the Met have created a simple present guide facility. You decide roughly how much you want to spend and which need meets the criteria the site offers. Out of the list of 12 items they suggested, for a present in the $75 region, the cufflinks and ties were more apposite than a rather obscure tome on hieroglyphics. There are copious details of delivery times, packaging details, corporate gifts, friends' schemes and the like within the shop areas. The level of online security and privacy seems high and, like the rest of the site, demonstrates a serious commitment to a full online experience.

Explore and Learn A link from the Museum's title page takes you into this area full of information, puzzles and educational resources. Many of the links are to information that appears elsewhere on the site (for example, some of the biographies of painters who appear here are also found in the special exhibitions sections) but the scale of the resource is impressive nonetheless. The main themes of the exhibition are discussed and even extended beyond the time frame of the original exhibit. There are similarly replete accounts of other themes and exhibitions, including, to name just two, the Art of Korea and American Folk Art. Within this section the Metropolitan introduces some games and puzzles specifically aimed at children.

Size, depth and sophistication all make this a site to come to for information and intellectual stimulus again and again.

www.ushmm.org/
United States Museum of the Holocaust

Overall rating: ★ ★ ★ ★ ★

Classification:	History museum	**Readability:**	★ ★ ★ ★ ★
Updating:	Monthly	**Content:**	★ ★ ★ ★ ★
Navigation:	★ ★ ★	**Speed:**	★ ★ ★

US 🔒

The United States Holocaust Memorial Museum has, in keeping with its subject matter, a sombre tone. Using an amazing and harrowing range of images, the site pulls no punches in its accounts of the suffering of the Jews during the Second World War.

It is impossible to fault the thoroughness of the approach and the high academic quality of the site. Although a visit to Belsen or Auschwitz may be more emotionally poignant, anyone seeking to understand the Holocaust could not find a better source of information or understanding than this site. It is really more of a resource and study centre than a museum; despite its online exhibits and accounts of the permanent galleries and temporary exhibitions, the bulk of the site is concerned with more strictly academic matters. There is a large online resource in the picture archive, and an option to search the library collections at the museum for archival material and books connected with the Holocaust. Both of these areas work quickly and effectively, though they should probably only be used as a guide to the nature of the collections rather than any indication of their size. It is difficult to see how any scholar or even university student could write about the Holocaust without examining this site closely. These facilities are complemented by the excellent online exhibitions, which contain many contemporary photos and documents.

This site represents more than just an archive, as all the research is ongoing and there is lots of information on job opportunities, fellowships, internships, education programs and the like. The site also acts as the homepage for a variety of societies and causes emerging from the Holocaust, such as Holocaust-era Assets, the Registry of Holocaust Survivors, and information about the proposed Holocaust Remembrance Day.

SPECIAL FEATURES

Picture Archive The picture archive contains a selection of some of the thousands of images held in store at the museum. Though the pictures can be viewed thematically, there is a search facility that works very well. Using a well-known Jewish surname produced harrowing pictures of a child of that name in a group photograph of a classroom from the early 1930s. All 20 children in the photo were named; that is the level of research that has gone into this site. The thematic display of contemporary images highlights this thoroughness; available online are 423 images of the concentration camps and 222 of women effected by the Holocaust.

Online Shop The shop contains a huge selection of books concerned with all aspects of the Holocaust and pre-war German history. There are hundreds of titles available, divided into sections corresponding to levels of interest and cross-referenced to particular themes. All have small descriptions, although there are few cover illustrations. The advanced study section contains much longer reviews, along with descriptions of some of the more recent and forthcoming publications. Delivery, payment methods and online security are painstakingly elaborated, and there would seem to be no better bookshop for this subject anywhere in the world.

Online Exhibition These exhibitions combine images and text in thought-provoking ways in order to cover specific aspects of the Holocaust and Nazism. Crystalnacht, the Berlin Olympics and the Holocaust in Greece are three examples of the nine themes. The carefully chosen images include rare photos, and the effect is both moving and informative. Much of the images in these presentations are merely photostats of administrative documents connected to the Final Solution or daily, governmental prejudice. These are presented in German with translations appearing over the top of the document in English. This method effectively demonstrates the intimate link between the apparatus of state and genocide; the minutiae of the administration required for murder and prejudice on such a scale is one of the most powerful concepts on the site. All the presentations run to about 20 pages in length and complement the work of the museum perfectly. Further details on each exhibition, including teaching packs, are available on request. This section also includes transcripts of some of the testimonies from the Nuremberg trials (with photos and in translation), as well as biographies of figures involved in the Holocaust and its aftermath.

Harrowing and shaming, this site deals massively well with one of the most horrific events in the history of Europe.

www.thebritishmuseum.ac.uk
The British Museum

Overall rating: ★ ★ ★ ★			
Classification:	History	Readability:	★ ★ ★
Updating:	Monthly	Content:	★ ★ ★ ★
Navigation:	★ ★ ★	Speed:	★ ★

This site has a glossiness and a huge, imposing size that you couldn't fail to find compelling. Moving through the plethora of links is quick and efficient. The images themselves are high in quality and stylishly lit, and the British Museum has for the next update of the site commissioned new and even higher quality photographs. There is an ongoing project to catalogue more of the objects within the collections as the site currently acts as a taster for the breadth of the collection. Still, even at the moment the sheer number and variety of the departments and their collections makes it difficult to keep track of everything there is to see and do on the site. This can make it quite difficult to pick out some of the masterpieces of the collection; perhaps for political reasons, some of the more contentious Classical and Egyptian objects do not appear at all. Mummies and the like do appear in the sophisticated online learning area, which contains tours, quizzes and games. These are all aimed at an indeterminate age, but there's enough breadth and detail here to satisfy most.

SPECIAL FEATURES

Online Shop The online shop is slick and easy to use. Although picture speed is still an issue, most of the items can be viewed in two different picture sizes, while the book covers of the more popular books also tend to be illustrated. If you are a fan of antiquated plaster and Past Times-style products you could spend hours in this area; however, the site has been careful to also have a decent selection of the more specialist publications available from the shop. Journal VI of Excavations at a 12th-century Blacksmith at Upper Wimbourne 1973-4 may not be to everyone's taste but it's to the museum's credit that they have kept some space for the more narrowly academic surfer. The transactions are assured security with powerful encryption software; clearer information on which credit cards are accepted would be useful. The electronic checkout does at least allow you to escape easily without the embarrassment of having your card refused. You can apply for a catalogue online and you will be sent confirmation by email, too. This seems to work efficiently; confirmation arrived the next day and the catalogue followed two days later.

Online Learning Aimed largely at children, the Online Learning section is full of fun and games. There are sections on various areas of Egyptian life, with challenges and tours related to both objects in the museum and their wider context. The challenges require a relatively painless download of software, and they are friendly and inviting. The idea of measuring the pyramids by using London buses speeding across the bottom of the screen is less childish and more fun than it may at first appear to be. The target age range for this is broad, while the traditional education area divides itself more distinctly with areas for adults and children.

Large, stately and refined, much like the museum itself.

www.getty.edu/museum/

The Getty Museum

Overall rating: ★ ★ ★ ★			
Classification:	Arts	Readability:	★ ★ ★ ★
Updating:	Monthly	Content:	★ ★ ★ ★ ★
Navigation:	★ ★	Speed:	★ ★ ★ ★ ★

(US)

This site has a wealth of information and images from probably the greatest private collection of art in the world. The site runs well, with images and search results appearing quickly. Given its sheer scale and complexity, it could take you a while to get to grips with the full potential of the site. The main cause of this is the homepage, which covers all the historical and artistic Getty projects as well as the museum itself. Given the number of foundations and charities supported by Getty, it is not surprising that the homepage has so much on it.

Following the links into the collection produces a well-designed page outlining three search options. Browsers can search for the works of a particular artist, search by theme or subject, or view the works by department. Although the artist search feature would be very useful for anyone interested in seeing the works of a particular artist, you should choose one of the themed tours to get a more spontaneous view of the collections. This wonderfully mimics the experience of strolling through the gallery and the sensation of reacting spontaneously to some of the world's finest pieces.

In addition to the objects, these tours provide a useful glossary and encyclopaedia of the subject. The mythology section, for example, contains an account of the development of various myths with depictions of them from Ancient Greek Vases; highlight any of the words and an explanation will instantly appear. Even the numerous characters from the Iliad become comprehensible through this approach.

Touring by department or object type can be a little daunting. This is, after all, one of the largest and most opulent private collections in the world, a fact fully represented on this site. The collection is of a size that seeing all the statues or even just the statues of animals can be numbing, even though all of them are well described with, again, many terms and references being defined. Anyone lucky enough to be researching subjects with relevance to the Getty collections could find information and objects quickly and efficiently using the site.

The calendar has a useful filter function so that you can elect to view only the lectures and tours connected with a specific area. Given the plethora of lectures, seminars and study days, this allows users to get a sensible idea of the variety and number of activities arranged by the Getty Museum.

SPECIAL FEATURES

Trajan's Column This online exhibition links Virtual Tours, static images and text to recreate the heart of early second-century Rome. Based around the surviving Trajan's Column, the forum is reconstructed in detail and the impact is impressive. Life around the forum is documented through more reconstructions and a scholarly text.

The online glossary and the range of artists covered make this a useful site for anyone with a serious interest in fine art.

www.tate.org.uk/
Tate Gallery, London

Overall rating: ★ ★ ★ ★			
Classification: Arts		**Readability:**	★ ★ ★ ★ ★
Updating: Monthly		**Content:**	★ ★ ★ ★ ★
Navigation: ★ ★ ★		**Speed:**	★ ★ ★

UK

This site exudes sophistication and modernity, so much so that it has even allowed a doppelganger site – called Mongrel – to be created by the Harwood. This achingly cool concept mimics components from the Tate site and creates new experiences and ideas with them.

The collection is described thematically, following the layout of many of the rooms, with themes such as The Portrait breaking down into individual rooms. This approach works well, each room receiving a description of its theme and the paintings' place in it. Below the description the paintings are listed with the artist and title details; clicking on either of these will bring up the online catalogue, where one can view the picture and explore other works by the artist. Given the number of images and artists, it's not surprising that these images don't expand to a great size. Servers only have so much memory and it is questionable whether people would wait for the download. Currently, it is quick and efficient. The catalogue of artists and their work is a marvel, containing details of almost the whole collection. While non-specialists will sample the 8,000 illustrated descriptions, those with a more in-depth interest can check 25,000 records for the works of their favourite artists.

SPECIAL FEATURES

Online Shop The shop is just as slick and modern as the rest of the site. The book catalogue is extensive without being huge, while each book cover is illustrated and, more importantly, has a two- or three-paragraph description. The range of posters, prints and postcards is vast, with almost the whole collection represented; unfortunately, the images can only be viewed as part of the collection database, so you have to remember the exact artist's details before ordering from the shop. The Tate has got round the lack of consumer confidence in online security by invoicing for the goods when an online order is received. This may feel more secure but it also makes the order and delivery process slower.

The Mongrel Opinion will be divided on the merit of this endeavour. We urge browsers to have a look, but beware: some of the images are quite distasteful. The general approach challenges authority and the canons of western art. The work of well-known artists is subverted by its partial or full replacement by grotesque images of decay and human bodies. Hogarth's work comes under a grotesque collage titled 'My Mom'. It depicts a face constructed out of portraiture and photographs of, presumably, the artist's mother. The pictures are accompanied with what look like excerpts from a history of the English penal system, specifically referring to the use of prison hulks in the 19th century. The concern is with the history of the English penal system, most notably its use of prison hulks in the Thames. Depending on your point of view, this is either a rather sick joke or a triumph in presenting alternative views of an established institution and its collections. Perhaps the artist should speak for himself: 'I have tried in this collection to play with the broken links within the Tate's collection, grafting on the skins of people who are close to me, dragging parts of the collection through the mud of the Thames, and infecting some of it with a relevant disease. This is a personal response to the cultural attitudes that I found within the aura of the collection.'

The Mongrel aside, this is a sophisticated site, covering Britain's premier collection of sculpture and paintings.

www.guggenheim.org
The Guggenheim Museum, New York

Overall rating: ★ ★ ★			
Classification:	History	Readability:	★ ★ ★
Updating:	Regular	Content:	★ ★
Navigation:	★ ★ ★ ★	Speed:	★ ★ ★

US 🔒

The quality of the images and the collections described on the homepage draw you into this ravishing site. Some of the high-definition images could perhaps have a bit more accompanying text but the histories of the unique Guggenheim building and its designer Frank Lloyd Wright are analysed in sumptuous detail. The wealth of detail is supplemented by links to the lectures schedule, which describes the various tours and lectures covering the design of this unique building. Follow the links to the exhibitions area for a full account including a wonderful 3D model of the proposed new Guggenheim Museum on the waterfront in Manhattan. Indeed, it is probably fair to say that the Guggenheim museum in New York is more concerned with its shell than its collections. The most interesting feature of the account of the new building's design and construction is the models depicting the building at various stages of completion. You can find them through the design diary link.

The exhibitions section contains a short, illustrated description of the permanent collection and the current temporary exhibition (Amazons of the Avant Garde when we visited the site). The description of the Special Programs is much fuller; surprisingly so, given the range of lectures, courses and seminars run by the foundation.

The site is well-designed and navigation works well. Generally, though, there is a sense of an opportunity missed. The shop is impressive but the details of the collection are sparse, not matching up to the museum's stature. One possible explanation is that the curators are keeping their powder dry and waiting for the further development of the virtual Guggenheim (see p. 108).

SPECIAL FEATURES

Museum Store The Guggenheim boasts a superb online store. The product range is large and pieces or artists from the collection inspire most of the objects. Everything is of a high quality and priced to match, especially the pieces in the collectors section. Some of the products are divided according to their potential use; for the home or the office, for example. Payment is accepted via all the usual credit cards and the level of security is as high as you'd expect from such an august institution.

A wonderful collection and setting, nicely explored and illustrated.

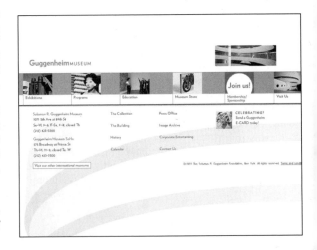

www.hermitagemuseum.org
Hermitage Palace

Overall rating: ★ ★ ★			
Classification:	History	Readability:	★ ★ ★ ★ ★
Updating:	Irregular	Content:	★ ★ ★ ★
Navigation:	★ ★ ★ ★	Speed:	★ ★

(RU)

The Hermitage site seems to sum up contemporary Russia; some quarters are thriving, modern and sophisticated, while others have yet to catch up. There are large, detailed and searchable sections on the collection and the building itself, plus an ambitious picture and object search facility. However, there is no real information about the shop (let alone an online store), ticketing, or facilities (cafes, loos and the like) as yet. Most importantly, though, the coverage of the collections and the objects is superb.

The digital picture bank is large and the quality of the images impressive, although the expandable link was not entirely reliable. Individual links from Scythian jewellery chains can be seen easily. Of course, the collection is first rate, so the objects deserve this level of quality and the online collection repays close study. In the Collection Highlights section, the choices are between traditional departments, such as Classical Antiquity, and discourses on the palaces or individuals rooms within them. All these pages have wonderfully full descriptions and commentaries on the collections or the building. They are accompanied by thumbnail images that are expandable and link to more detailed descriptions of the individual objects. Given the range of the collection – from Palaeolithic sculpture to 19th-century rifles – there should be something here to interest most.

At the top of each page there is an intriguing series of rolling headlines from news stories concerning the museum. Click on them for a summary of whatever the issue or occasion is. Many of these refer to the opening or closing of a new exhibition at the Hermitage or one of its many exciting, travelling exhibitions. The number of these exhibitions betokens the significance of the museum's collections. Each of the current exhibitions, though not those past or forthcoming, has a link to pages describing its content, its itinerary (if it's a travelling exhibition) and its dates.

SPECIAL FEATURES

Online Search The Hermitage has one of the most successful search features of this kind for any of the major museums. The search engine pulls up images and text quickly and easily. There are quite detailed notes to help any user narrow a search, but the basic search feature pulled up information using some fairly obscure terms of reference. The QBIC search facility is a special project of IBM, and it works by finding colours or shapes in pictures. Using a simple colour chart or drawing programme, you can search the Hermitage's collection for paintings with similar use of colour or construction. Results are shown in order of relevance. The initial results are impressive, but some of the later suggestions seem to bear little relation to the colour or shape being searched for. When it's complete, this facility should become a staple of all museums with large collections of paintings; as it is, it is worth trying but more for fun than for research.

The wonderfully varied collections of this vast, international collection are well-represented on this ambitious site.

www.vam.ac.uk
Victoria & Albert Museum

Overall rating: ★ ★ ★			
Classification:	History	Readability:	★ ★ ★ ★
Updating:	Monthly	Content:	★ ★ ★ ★
Navigation:	★ ★	Speed:	★ ★ ★

UK

Befitting its status as one of the foremost design museums in the world the V&A site has an ultra-modern feel and look. Cubes of images revolve and flash, enticing viewers into a series of special features, exhibitions and gallery tours. So stylishly designed is the site that it can be difficult not to ignore the details of locations and opening times.

The shop shares the same slick design and feel as the rest of the site, although there is no real online shop, as such; orders are taken via email or phone. The product range is very good for books, boasting cover shots and brief descriptions of the contents. However, the range in the gifts section doesn't capture the elegance or breadth of the products available in the shops within the museum itself. The broad range of books covers all aspects of the collection, representing a very useful resource for anyone seriously studying design or art history. Of related interest is the link to the National Art Library site (www.nal.vam.ac.uk/), which offers about 300,000 titles on its searchable library. This facility works well, connecting users directly to the OPAC (Search) facility. Search results appear surprisingly quickly.

SPECIAL FEATURES

Online Gallery The V&A boasts a searchable online catalogue of 2,000 objects from the collection. Objects can be searched for using keywords, countries, periods, or categories. For example, searching for Spain will lead you to 16th-century glassware and 15th-century armour. The approach works well, giving a good idea of the range and complexity of the collections. Captioned images appear quickly, considering the quality of the pictures, and the overall effect is not unlike strolling through the galleries, with objects catching your eye as you go.

Explorer You could easily miss this beautiful map and gallery guide, given the other links on the homepage. Choosing the actual tour link on the homepage produces a three-dimensional image of the building's interior. This corresponds to a list of the gallery headings on the left-hand side of the page. Moving over the physical space highlights the relevant gallery entry, while clicking on the gallery entry highlights the physical space. The effect is more exciting than the usual two-dimensional plan with hotlinks to text. Having found the relevant gallery, click on it to see a short description as well as links to selected highlights of the gallery. Objects appear quickly in high-quality images that fill half the screen. Harder to describe than to use, the Explorer feature is a unique form of virtual tour that gives a wonderful sense of the museum's interior spaces.

Virtual Galleries Virtual Galleries is a rather catch-all term on this site, and this area would be better described as an online forum. Much of the material is derived from personal responses to the art. The V&A has encouraged people to react to their collection through the creation of websites and posters, both of which can be found here. The posters are generally more successful than the websites, but both make one think about the collection in a new way; more importantly, none of it is as potentially offensive as the content of the Mongrel spart of the Tate's site.

The biggest design museum in the world has an incredibly designed (some might say over-designed) site that is worth exploring for some unique features.

OTHER SITES OF INTEREST

George Pompidou Centre, France
www.centrepompidou.fr/
A very glossy yellow dominates this site, which gives visiting details and overviews of the building, its history and its aims. The philosophy behind the museum's collections and exhibitions are described, although no details of current exhibitions appear. Still, the images are good and it all looks suitably stylish. The work of the individual departments is explained with a few stray titbits about the study collections. There is a lot more material here – including press kits and exhibition details – for those who speak French.

German Historical Museum, Berlin
www.dhm.de/index.html
Scroll down on reaching the homepage to click on the British flag for an English version. This museum covers German art and history from about the 11th century, providing a wealth of information and background detail to make it worth a view before any visit to Berlin. There is an online shop taking credit card orders; the current range of English titles is small but German readers will find lots of exhibition catalogues and more general titles. There is a searchable database of objects within the museum that works well, provided you are not put off by the German directions and titles.

Museo Napoleonico, Rome
www.comune.roma.it/museonapoleonico
Though only available in French or Italian, this site merits attention because it's an exciting museum and collection for anyone feeling a little jaded with churches and the Roman Empire. Unlike many of the other Italian sites, it has lots of information and some high-quality images. Napoleonic history is a staple of the fiction and non-fiction best-sellers list but here, instead of warfare, we have an intimate portrayal of the amazing family that produced five crowned heads of Europe. This museum documents their lives through miniatures, all in a stunning architectural setting.

Vatican Museums
www.vatican.va/phome_en.htm
Direct from Vatican City, this is the official papal website. Pope John Paul II (himself a silver surfer) endorsed the validity of information technology, and its potential applications for the Roman Catholic Church. This site is a work in progress, into which substantial resources are still being invested. Content is currently available in English, German, French, Portuguese, Spanish and Italian versions (with some Polish input). The Holy Father, as one would expect, has a host of resources online. Archives include encyclicals, apostolic letters, homilies, and speeches. There are also links to the weekly Vatican newpaper, radio programmes and press releases relating to the pope. Unfortunately, the section entitled Museums still seems to be in the developmental stage, and currently stands empty. So, if you're looking for a site that represents all the activities of the Vatican, this website is a half-empty chalice, or half-full, depending on your perspective. Given time, it will hopefully develop but at present the site is best viewed as an online museum devoted to the Pope.

Chapter 02

animal, vegetable and mineral

This chapter is devoted to those museums that we all looked forward to being dragged around as school children. Museums dedicated to history and art tend to instil boredom, or if not that, at least fear inspired by the warders. These are the museums that set out to encourage children to explore and, occasionally, learn. The sub-heading to this chapter could well have been 'for the children'. Indeed, the websites that we review here, typically, have far more content aimed at children than some more highbrow museums have in their specifically child-orientated sections. Generally, these museums have a high level of activity within their physical galleries that is usually reflected on their websites.

These are the museums that children rush around, pushing all the buttons and embarrassing their parents with questions on issues that most parents remember having once known enough about to pass an exam. Fortunately, most of those in this section have enough 'knobs and whistles' to keep children away from asking basic scientific questions of their parents. Most of the websites have a similar aim, with lots of games and interactives masked as learning and, occasionally, lots of learning masked as an interactive or a game. Forming an honourable exception to this trend is the Oxford Museum of Science, which we have included because it demonstrates that the history of science does not need to be consistently explained in a vocabulary designed for those under 15 years of age.

This doesn't tell the whole story, of course. The pleasure of the internet is that you can reach all sorts of different audiences within one site; hence the proliferation of children's trails, areas and the like. As well as being child-friendly, many of the sites in this section have a distinguished academic core, representing substantial repositories of knowledge and information on the web.

Ongoing research projects appear on the UK Science and Natural History museum websites, and it is common for the American institutions to publish magazines or conference proceedings largely or wholly online.

www.nhm.ac.uk/
The Natural History Museum

Overall rating: ★ ★ ★ ★ ★			
Classification:	Natural history	Readability:	★ ★ ★ ★
Updating:	Regularly	Content:	★ ★ ★ ★
Navigation:	★ ★ ★	Speed:	★ ★

UK

The Natural History Museum proudly boasts that its website went online in 1994, making it the first UK museum to have a website. Certainly its scale and complexity befits its age. There are numerous virtual tours, images, databases, interactives, fact files and even a video feed from an ant colony. The Ant Cam can only be accessed by ten browsers at once, but it is worth the wait – the life of the ants is surprisingly compelling.

The navigation is generally very good but if you're looking for anything specific, be sure to use the quick and effective search facility. The site map, though large and complex, is generally easy to find. The download speed is generally high, with images appearing quickly.

The museum's digital picture library seems to be a very impressive resource, with 8,500 images and growing according to the blurb, which must represent a significant proportion of the displayed collection. You can search by keywords or subject and, as a mark of its functionality, the 'early man' section contains 175 images of reconstructions, drawings and skeletons. The descriptions are technical rather than analytical, so they are more for the specialist or enthusiast than the general visitor. Certainly the quality of the images and the fact that they are easily expandable would allow certain kinds of preliminary research to be done online. There are extensive details for those who wish to purchase these images for reproduction or printing, but a distinct lack of such details for those wishing to purchase from the large shop within the museum.

There is no online shop as yet, but the site says they are building one and will email before one is created with special 'online only bargains'. Given the success in the UK of the Natural History Museum's mail-order business, this is a surprising omission.

Some of the museum's website is devoted to quite technical subjects which will be beyond the general browser, but for the caterpillar-obsessed individual who didn't know before, the NHM is the centre for a worldwide Caterpillar Hostplants database. In a similar vein, the department runs a Host Parasite Database to which queries can be emailed, the extensive protocols for which are outlined. There are other examples of the site supporting significant academic endeavour and it is pleasing to see that, unlike some institutions, the museum hasn't gone entirely down the astronauts-and-monsters-for-kids route.

SPECIAL FEATURES

Interactives Ant Cam is a wonderful idea which makes the lives of the museum's colony of leaf cutter ants accessible for 24 hours a day. Both video feed and static images that change every ten seconds are available, depending on your patience and the speed of your modem. An online exhibition recounts the voyages of Captain Cook's ship The Endeavour. This works well, although be aware that you need to click on the text rather than the images to follow the link. There are plans of the Endeavour ship (with QuickTime views of rooms within), details of his route, small biographies of his captains, and information on some of the native flora and fauna. None of this is long or detailed, but it would provide a starting point for those trying to drum up enthusiasm in a school project for those up to the age of about ten.

Quest This online experience allows browsers to interrogate certain items from the collection. They can be viewed from numerous angles, measured, weighed and 'touched'. You can also ask a museum expert about them, all with a view to publishing your findings about the object on the web. All this conforms to the UK National Education Guidelines, so it is suitably righteous, even though it could work a little faster. Reading through the notes that previous visitors have left, other surfers seem to have enjoyed the experience.

Earth Lab You can find as much or as little as you ever wanted to know about geology here. Using many of the displays from the permanent exhibition, this section describes how rocks change and the effect this has had on our world. More specifically, it boasts a massive database of rock and fossil samples, which you can search using a variety of criteria. If you've visited the gallery and want to explore in more detail, you could spend hours here.

Lots for the little scientist in everyone and as much for the big scientist that no one wants to grow up into.

www.amnh.org
The American Museum of Natural History

Overall rating: ★ ★ ★ ★			
Classification:	History	**Readability:**	★ ★ ★ ★ ★
Updating:	Monthly	**Content:**	★ ★ ★ ★ ★
Navigation:	★ ★ ★	**Speed:**	★ ★ ★

US

The American Museum of Natural History boasts an enormous site, fully reflecting the complexity and variety of life on this planet. There is so much material that surfing through the pages and links can become bewildering; you start looking for Tyrannosaurus teeth and halfway through you've decided that the online exhibition on evolution looks more interesting. Some of the special exhibitions are discussed below (only the current ones) but the same level of sophistication can be found in much of the gallery information. For example, while casually surfing the Fossil Hall you can follow a link to an electronic newspaper that is full of contemporary fossils and theories, as well as three-dimensional studies of skeletons and fossils. The same sort of information is available within the online gallery itself.

The online shop was being redeveloped when we visited the site, but when completed it should offer a wide range of goods of a similar type to those found in the UK's Science and Natural History Museums.

SPECIAL FEATURES

Fighting Dinosaurs of Mongolia Using video clips, virtual tours, FAQs and an image gallery, this online exhibition contains a vast amount of information on dinosaurs, their lives and their typologies. Given our increasingly dinosaur-obsessed world, this must be one of the museum's most visited areas. Anyone looking to push their knowledge beyond Hollywood films and cartoons could very profitably spend time in this area of the site.

Rose Centre for Earth and Space Through images, film clips and text, this area explores the nature of the universe and the physical constants within it. Concepts ranging in scale from atoms to galaxies are described in depth and the overall effect is impressive. Most of the images and moving footage runs in Windows Media players, so few downloads should be needed. Note that many of the clips have sound so be sure to have your speakers on. The Rose Centre also has a full-size Planetarium that, from the description and some digital images, looks impressive indeed. Tickets for the showings throughout the day can be purchased by credit card online.

Natural History This is the online version of the monthly natural history magazine produced by the museum every month. There are digests and extracts from the articles appearing in each issue, as well as one featured article reproduced in full. Stimulating browsers to buy your product as well as visit your museum and, in effect, giving them something for nothing seems to be a brilliant model to follow. If you are interested in the Natural History of Biology, bookmark this site and there will be something new for you every month.

A site that successfully combines serious scholarship with lots of fun new media touches.

www.mhs.ox.ac.uk/

Museum of the History of Science, Oxford

Overall rating: ★ ★ ★ ★

Classification:	Science	**Readability:**	★ ★ ★ ★ ★
Updating:	Monthly	**Content:**	★ ★ ★ ★
Navigation:	★ ★ ★	**Speed:**	★ ★ ★

UK

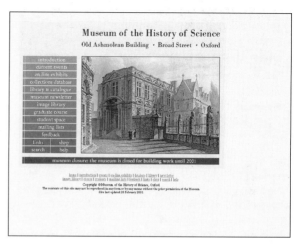

This museum suffers somewhat from geography; it is set back from Oxford Street and tourists flood past it to gape at attractions such as The Sheldonian and various locations from Inspector Morse programs. Consequently, it is pleasing to see that it enjoys a luxuriant website. Unlike most of the other science museums with a web presence, the intellectual and artistic tone is high. You can search the collection for 16th-century mathematical texts or read about the role of biblical scholarship in the development of science. It is most definitely not kids playing noisily with springs. Some idea of the wealth and scope of material on the site can be gauged by the On-line Exhibits, which are superb online realisations of the recent exhibitions held at the museum.

Though much of the museum is currently closed for renovation and extension work, the museum authorities have put a couple of QuickTime tours in, to allow surfers to witness the renovations. It's certainly a novel approach; instead of having an indifferent image of some showcases, this museum has good quality images of a white-washed room containing some builders' paraphernalia, or a large hole on Broad Street with some larger builders' equipment.

SPECIAL FEATURES

On-line Exhibits The background to these exhibits varies widely over the history of science and society. Early photographers, gunners, astronomers and mathematicians all feature in essays that are full of intelligent and in-depth text, including apposite images. Of note to anyone planning a visit to Oxford is the charming final exhibit, the Virtual Oxford Science Walk. Using engravings and maps, this tour explains to visitors the developing history of science at Oxford and the numerous startling discoveries that have taken place there. The careers of a variety of figures – from the 13th-century Doctor Mirabilis, Roger Bacon, to Stephen Hawking – are elucidated as part of the history and architecture of Oxford.

A serious and scholarly site for those with a more-than-passing interest in the history of science.

www.nmpft.org.uk/

National Museum of Photography, Film and Television

Overall rating: ★ ★ ★ ★

Classification:	Museum	Readability:	★ ★ ★ ★
Updating:	Regular	Content:	★ ★ ★ ★
Navigation:	★ ★ ★	Speed:	★ ★

UK

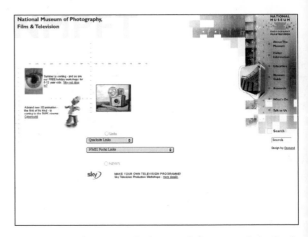

As you would expect from this Bradford-based museum's concern with image, the homepage of their website is highly polished; a disembodied runner careers across the screen and a variety of noises that settle into music accompany him. Once all this is done, the homepage is delightfully designed, with navigation by menus in the centre and on the left-hand side of the page. The pages load smoothly and the practical information is seamless.

The vast collections and archives are described with a genuine enthusiasm for all things photographic and filmic. The collections are divided between media and format, so feature films are separated from soap operas, which is a good thing. Among a vast film and photographic archive, such oddities as Javanese Shadow Puppets and Ursula Andrews's makeup for the 1965 film She are just part of an intriguing and constantly surprising mix of objects.

Much of the text within the site contains links to biographies, photos and film clips, including the earliest known moving footage. Bizarrely this is a somewhat dull clip of Leeds bridge. The collections and archives are fully described; researchers or those with an unhealthy interest in TV and film trivia could doubtless spend hours here.

The education section is split according to age and educational level. Film Studies courses are run from the

museum and many of the modules are described. Information packs, teaching aids, special events and lectures are all offered in very full detail and range, though try to avoid the section called The Dead because the title is unforgivingly accurate.

Slick and thoroughly competent, this site has much to offer both casual browsers and those with particular interests in film and photographic history.

www.phm.gov.au/
The Power House

Overall rating: ★ ★ ★ ★			
Classification:	National site	Readability:	★ ★ ★ ★
Updating:	Unclear	Content:	★ ★ ★ ★
Navigation:	★ ★ ★	Speed:	★ ★ ★

AUS

Though navigation is clumsy (you have to click and wait for the link to go red), this site has a lot of potential, covering as it does a prolific collection and a unique series of special exhibitions. The permanent galleries are an eclectic mix, with exhibitions on Brewing and Pubs sitting next to Space Exploration and the Strasbourg clock. The coverage of specific exhibitions can be patchy but the breadth and variety of the collection (vacuum cleaners to Coptic textiles) is such that the lack of coherent coverage is understandable.

Follow the Online Web Projects link for virtual tours of more detailed coverage of areas in the museum. Exhibitions on Star Trek and the history of circuses in Australia give some flavour of the content.

Potentially a very good site, and the best from the antipodes.

www.nmsi.ac.uk/science_museum_fr.htm
The Science Museum

Overall rating: ★ ★ ★ ★			
Classification:	Science	Readability:	★ ★ ★ ★
Updating:	Monthly	Content:	★ ★ ★ ★
Navigation:	★ ★ ★	Speed:	★ ★

UK

This large site has some wonderful touches and is generally sharp and well-designed. Links work with precision and speed, operating either via the highlighted words in the text or the menus that generally appear on the left-hand side of each page. The overall structure is large and complex, with links flowing out from the homepage. The homepage is actually more like a news page, dealing largely with the most recent events and happenings at the museums. But if you can fight past them follow the collections link on the left-hand side of the homepage. Here you can find out about the permanent collections by subject and then by theme or gallery (be sure to click on the title, not the image). These pages explore all the facets of the Museum's extensive galleries and collections. All the information here is illustrated and much of it is linked to the English National Curriculum, so is suitable for children's projects.

The Science Museum's online shop is currently quite small; when we first visited the site, it wasn't up at all. This is surprising given the success of the mail-order business. The products tend to be zany – a see-through camera is a typical example – but well-designed, and the online ordering is done on a secure server.

SPECIAL FEATURES

Online Exhibitions This uses a series of interactives to explain a variety of issues and concepts. The Apollo 11 exhibition, for example, has quite an inventive leaning game about building rockets, a VR tour of the inside of Apollo 11 and video clips featuring the crew members. Doubtless to the joy of sci-fi fans, Arthur C Clarke has his own exhibition. (No interactives, though, only text and images.) Also featured are 'exhiblets', which we saw at the National Railway Museum. These tend to be smaller, without any interactivity built into them, but they do present information in an attractive way.

The Wellcome Wing On first glimpse, this pumps contemporary dance music at you in a nod to its self-aware modernity. Unfortunately, the rest of this area doesn't work quite as well as it might, as the choice of downloads or plug-ins required to view the virtual tour are too complex and too slow. Choose which will suit your PC (go for the first option in the list, if you're unsure – it's the simplest) and then click on OK to confirm the downloads. Once loaded and operational, the tour works well; you can actually move around rather than turn on the spot, as well as zoom in and out. Displays and computers appear in rather poor detail, but if you click on them the concept behind them is displayed and discussed. Since most of this gallery in based on personal experiments and knowledge, much of the experience is lost on the web. For instance, one of the machines enables you to collect your iris and voice pattern but only if you're standing in front of it, although the results are saved onto your own personal website, created for you at the Museum and hosted by them.

High-tech and heavily aimed at children but with some depth for the more adult.

www.cite-sciences.fr/english/
La Villette, City of Science

Overall rating: ★ ★ ★ ★			
Classification:	Science	**Readability:**	★ ★ ★
Updating:	Regularly	**Content:**	★ ★ ★ ★
Navigation:	★ ★ ★	**Speed:**	★ ★ ★

(FR)

Like the museum itself, this site is full of interactivity and novel displays. It's slightly more sophisticated, with better navigation and a more pleasing graphical style, than the English Science Museum, and a real powerhouse of a site. Film clips, games, virtual tours and story boards all combine to produce a website in which there is always something you haven't seen yet. Navigation can be a little tricky though, as new options pop up on the homepage when you click on the option you thought you wanted. The site is fully integrated with the museum and keeps track of the copious daily happenings (lectures, films, experiments) at the Science centre. Curiously, there is no online store, as La Villette itself has a wonderfully large and exciting shop. One issue to note is that some areas of the site are available only in French. This isn't that much of a problem except for technical and navigation information, which we found to be a nightmare.

SPECIAL FEATURES

The Invisible The Invisible can be found by following the Look link from the homepage. The premise of this area is the importance of the atomic structure of objects. Click on the icons depicting wood and similar materials to open a window and start a voiceover. The image is magnified again and again with the camera panning over its surface as the disembodied voice describes what we're looking at. The effect is impressive and stimulating.

Virtual Tours The French have picked up a trick which should have been noticed by the other museums that take the RealPlayer tour approach: they have linked several tours together so that you get a genuine sense of movement. As you scroll around the screen, look for the cursor to change into an open door. Double clicking on it will take you through into the next part of the tour. Starting outside the magnificent glass building, the tour zooms through the large forums and walkways within La Villette. There is even a large-scale view that almost fills the screen and works much better than the usual small screen version. For those with lots of patience or time on their hands, there is a net cam showing the main atrium of the site; given that it only changes every minute and the download is slow, though, you may be better off with the RealPlayer tours.

Virtual Encyclopaedia These illustrate various processes within the body and also astronomical concepts. Typically they run in a RealPlayer window for about a minute and they appear and download quickly. Subject matter includes digestion, growing, the skeleton, satellites and comets. The accidentally comic tone may irritate some but there is enough information to hold a child's attention. La Villette claims to be adding ten new films a month. Given the success of these, surfers should check back often to see what has been added.

An eclectic combination of features and information make this a powerful site, sure to fascinate children.

www.eureka.org.uk
Eureka

Overall rating: ★ ★ ★			
Classification: Science		**Readability:**	★ ★ ★ ★ ★
Updating: Varies		**Content:**	★ ★ ★
Navigation: ★ ★ ★ ★ ★		**Speed:**	★ ★ ★ ★

UK

Eureka's vast museum in Halifax introduces young children to science and technology via its giant-sized interactive models, activities and workshops.

The website is a little more compact, and unlike many other children's museums, it has avoided the interactive approach, instead opting for a straightforward representation of what the museum has to offer. However, it is no less worthy an attempt because of this, and presents an enticing snippet of what a day out at Eureka will involve, successfully whetting your appetite.

SPECIAL FEATURES

Welcome to Eureka explains the Eureka experience. To access the section, click on the link to the right of the dog, at the bottom of the homepage.

News and Events highlights regular Eureka activities such as Storytime Saturdays, as well as special limited-term events like international exhibitions and interactive family workshops.

Teacher Planning explains how teachers can utilise Eureka's resources for children at Key Stage one and two. There are examples of School-trip itineraries and Curriculum Links, which indicate the exhibits particularly relevant to specific aspects of the curriculum.

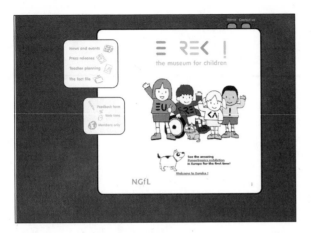

Fact File gives Opening times, admission fees and intructions on how to get there.

A simple site explaining the Eureka experience.

www.msim.org.uk/
The Museum of Science & Industry, Manchester

Overall rating: ★ ★ ★			
Classification:	Science	Readability:	★ ★ ★
Updating:	Monthly	Content:	★ ★ ★
Navigation:	★ ★ ★	Speed:	★ ★

UK

This site is quite strikingly slick and space age, with phaser-like noises that rush at you as you follow the links (tip: turn the sound down). If you've got a sluggish PC, choose the option from the homepage to view the site without Flash. Some of the high-tech effect won't work but the site will run much more quickly. Generally the links work quickly and smoothly but care must be taken with the navigation; the links are rather sensitive and only appear with options when the cursor is hovered over them. QuickTime player is used widely but we had some difficulties with the more up-to-date downloads. Once QuickTime is installed there are lots of good video clips, some of them up to ten minutes long. The download of the video feed is remarkably quick.

SPECIAL FEATURES

The Hands On Section This is little more than a gratuitous use of games to promote children's interest in the site, but there's no real harm in that. The range of games is good and, though lacking in much scientific or industrial background, they are stimulating and challenging. Certainly Racing Circuits proved a little too challenging for this author.

Transport This section contains film footage (QuickTime) and virtual reality tours, by which you can examine virtual trains, pistons and the like. The virtual viewer can be difficult to use at first; the trick is to hover the cursor over the buttons. A title will then appear over them, telling you what each does. These films are an intriguing mix of the abstract and the informative.

Video Clips The site wallows in film clips. Many are much longer than are normally found on museum sites, and they are used cogently. Highlights include an astronaut's demonstration of Newtonian physics and a 1930s view of what the home of the future would be like. Note that if you change the size of the windows you can run the film clips while you get on with other kinds of work.

A busy and thriving site, full of toys which can be used for whiling away the time and learning about science.

OTHER SITES OF INTEREST

Blanding Dinosaur Museum, USA
www.dinosaur-museum.org/
Based in Utah, a centre for dinosaur discoveries, this museum's site has much for any members of the legion of people fascinated by dinosaurs. Images and online exhibitions describe the work of the museum as well as the lives and habits of the Cretaceous at this website. Be sure to click on all the pictures, as many expand into larger images and act as links to further pages which can be difficult to find if you only follow the highlighted links.

Chapter 03

paintings and fine art

The emphasis here is on Art or, to some, fine art; or, to others, 'proper art'. What people mean by such terms is anyone's guess, but this chapter is basically concerned with representation, whether on canvas or in stone, wood, flesh or whatever else a modern artist uses in an attempt to shock. Goyas, Rembrandts and Van Goghs, accompanied by many lesser-known artists, form the leading lights of the collections in this chapter. Modern art, in all its fecundity, is also well represented.

Though many of the world's most famous paintings are held by the great international museums – and have therefore been covered in Chapter One – the collections here are those that are splendid in their depth rather than in their general range. The Louvre has the Mona Lisa and a smattering of other works by Renaissance artists, but it lacks the wealth of Flemish painting that the Rijksmuseum possesses. Similarly, where else in the world can we see the gathering of Van Gogh's work that we find at the Van Gogh Museum? Of course, painting is but one aspect of the artist's oeuvre, and sculpture also figures highly in the collections of the museums in this section. This is particularly true of the modern art museums, for which there is often no real distinction between paintings, sculpture and installation art.

www.npg.org.uk
National Portrait Gallery

Overall rating: ★ ★ ★ ★ ★

Classification:	Arts	Readability:	★ ★ ★
Updating:	Monthly	Content:	★ ★ ★ ★ ★
Navigation:	★ ★	Speed:	★ ★ ★ ★

UK

Despite many of its most high-profile portraits being as old as the 16th century, the online National Portrait Gallery oozes modernity and chic. This is partly due to a major new redisplay and program of renovation, well documented on the site. The interactive map (meaning only that it has links to information and images from the collection) is effective, displaying the depth and breadth of the collection. Beyond the information in the gallery guides there is a lot more text, along with analysis of the collections and paintings.

Accounts of previous exhibitions appear in the Press Release section, in the Education section and, for forthcoming exhibitions, in the Publications section. A long history of the museum is buried in the Questions section; this has information about exhibitions that are also found in the What's New Section. This rather random approach keeps the site novel but can make it difficult to find specific information about specific exhibitions. Still, it does keep you looking.

The Shop has a limited presence online; orders can be emailed or printed out and faxed. The product range, described with pictures and brief descriptions, is small but well thought-out and attractively designed, so it is a pity that you cannot order online. However, if you use the search engine and its database of images, the museum shop does offer a unique service. Any of the images within the collection can be printed out using a high-quality poster printer within the shop. The Publications section contains long(ish) descriptions of various recent and forthcoming publications which would be useful to art students, but these cannot even be ordered by email or fax.

SPECIAL FEATURES

Online Search The National Portrait Gallery boasts one of the most comprehensive and effective online search engines among all the national and international museums. It claims to have over 10,000 pictures displayed online, and even a quick play with the search engine seems to confirm this amount. Like the gallery descriptions, the images are unfortunately still only thumbnail size. Still, the suggestions offered by the search engine are always coherent, and the collection can be searched by painter, subject, theme, date or style. The size of the collection means that the number of images offered in result for any search is surprisingly high. One would expect the Duke of Wellington as a national hero to appear a few times, but the collection has 17 images, many of them not on regular display (including sketches and, rather startlingly, a clay death mask). The variety of portraits is undermined by the lack of any real description or analysis of the pictures, though those that appear in the gallery sections do have descriptions in those areas.

An amazingly comprehensive search engine gives this museum probably the largest online collection in the world.

www.nationalgallery.org.uk
National Gallery

Overall rating: ★ ★ ★ ★			
Classification:	Arts	Readability:	★ ★ ★ ★
Updating:	Regular	Content:	★ ★ ★ ★ ★
Navigation:	★ ★ ★ ★ ★	Speed:	★ ★ ★ ★
UK			

London's National Gallery enjoys a particularly slick website, with all the pictures illustrated and the site map displaying a large, well thought-out scheme. The highlights of the collection are presented in 12 selected works. There is also a selection called Puzzling Pictures, which have some mystery or oddity associated with them. These oddities are engaging, and by following the interpretation offered a non-specialist browser would develop a greater appreciation of the art historian's craft. In a similar vein, there is a games section in which one has to match two halves of a character from a painting. It's an amusing way of passing 10 minutes but nothing more serious than that. Certainly children's interests do not feature very highly; there are currently no details in the schools exhibitions area. The Museum News centre is a lot more informative, and its combination of bright images and upbeat text has an engaging feel.

The Gallery's catalogue is impressive, even if greater effort could perhaps be made to group the works by theme or period. By contrast, the paintings in the temporary exhibitions receive a long description of their thematic coherence, forming an attractive, stimulating introduction to any of the subjects covered. Recent themes have included French Impressionism 1860-90, and Vermeer and the Delft School. Usefully they have similarly full treatments of upcoming exhibitions, so browsers could plan a visit to coincide with an exhibition that had particularly caught their attention. Tickets for the temporary exhibitions are available online, using credit cards for payment. Rather oddly, though, given the level of recent investment in the Sainsbury Wing Shop, there is no online store or even catalogue. Instead, browsers are encouraged to email or telephone their request to the mail-order department.

SPECIAL FEATURES

Online Gallery This searchable (by artist, work or accession number) gallery contains the full catalogue of the museum's holdings. Pleasingly, all are illustrated and given descriptions and analysis. Unlike many of the major national museums, the objects are usefully analysed when shown on the web, rather than just captioned. Artists are displayed alphabetically and careful distinctions are drawn between the artist, his followers and his school. Of slight concern is the size of the images: they appear as thumbnails and are expandable to only about six by seven inches, but then larger images would take longer to download. The National Gallery is a member of the Euro Gallery Project; hopefully, all the other members and projected members will have an online catalogue of the same standard as is found here.

A massive collection of art from all periods and schools is well-represented on the National Gallery's Site.

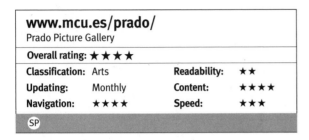

www.mcu.es/prado/
Prado Picture Gallery

Overall rating: ★ ★ ★ ★			
Classification: Arts		**Readability:**	★★
Updating:	Monthly	**Content:**	★★★★
Navigation:	★★★★	**Speed:**	★★★

SP

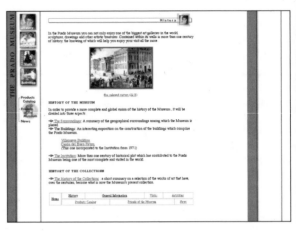

The Prado museum is famous for its paintings collection, which spans the 16th to the 19th century. Consequently, the paintings catalogue rates as easily the best bit of this website. Each month an individual painting is analysed in considerable detail, with very instructive results. A similar amount of care is taken with the sections describing the history of the museum's collections and architecture. The text lists dates, facts and events; some personalities discussed have links to their portraits, and it is difficult to imagine a fuller explanation of the museum's history. The visiting information is full and useful, even if it does have the rather odd title of Visiting File. Indeed, the whole site suffers from some peculiarities of expression or, more realistically, translation. In some cases, these are quite charming.

There is so much on the site that it is forgivable that some of the more complicated technical features don't work as well as they might. On some occasions, the online search for paintings, cross-referenced by period, style and country, produced a string of error codes (some in Spanish) and no results. To be fair, on subsequent visits the search worked very well, producing pertinent and accurate results.

SPECIAL FEATURES

Fine Art Lesson This series of online tutorials constitutes a fine way of imparting information and interest in the techniques of painting analysis. After an initial description including the historical background, the viewer is directed to study particular areas of a painting, such as motifs, areas of shadow, posture and so on. Unlike some museums where such features are only created once – or lapse so that monthly updates become yearly – it is clear from the list of images to view and study that a new picture has been chosen each month. The paintings selected reflect the wide range of styles and periods covered by the collection.

A wonderful collection described in great detail, and marred only by some technical faults.

www.rijksmuseum.nl
Rijksmuseum

Overall rating: ★ ★ ★ ★			
Classification:	Arts	**Readability:**	★ ★ ★
Updating:	Monthly	**Content:**	★ ★ ★ ★
Navigation:	★ ★ ★ ★	**Speed:**	★ ★ ★ ★

NL

Available in a number of languages, this site has more than 6,000 pages of text, 4,000 illustrations and 150 QuickTime tours (according to the designers!). All of these work speedily and, with the exception of some links on the homepage, navigation is easy. Don't be put off by the slightly confusing English introduction page, which features a cropped detail from what looks like a Reubens. Unfortunately, you have to move the cursor over this image before any of the further options appear. There is another set at the top of the page so it would be quite easy to miss the virtual tour, the Glory of the Golden Age or the latest news from the Rijksmuseum. Beyond these options, those along the top of the screen allow access to the online shop, the history news of the museum, future exhibitions, and descriptions of the collection.

The museum runs a very full calendar, with events every day and film showings almost every half hour. If you're planning a visit, be sure to check the calendar heading to find out what is on a specific day. Just click on the specific date and all the options should come up. Ticket requests for future exhibitions can be emailed to the relevant local agent; a list is provided on the site.

SPECIAL FEATURES

Virtual Tour There are virtual tours for each room in the collection, which must have taken simply ages to do. The usual caveats about QuickPlayer tours apply (image quality, download speed), though care seems to have been taken to have the rooms lit properly. Sensibly, the Virtual Tour screens have a series of links to images and descriptions of the highlights of the collection.

Online Collection Database Themes, techniques and the history of art are described through the analysis of 12,500 objects from the collection. Concepts marked in yellow can be clicked and definitions appear; thus, an entry for Dürer also provides descriptions of Classicism and the Renaissance as artistic concepts. These may well be beneath some people but, by contrast, the shadow and light in Rembrandt's famous Night Watch painting is rigorously analysed over 12 screens of images and text.

Online Store Given the speed of the rest of the site, it is surprising how consistently slow the shop pages were to load. It features more than 100 items, and payment is via encrypted credit card details. Orders are despatched within two weeks and the whole operation has an air of efficiency about it. Still, the product range is good, featuring images of all the products, even if some of the design is a little odd.

As befits the national museum for a country that is only known for its paintings and its flowers, this site is brilliant for paintings.

www.vangoghmuseum.nl

Van Gogh Museum

Overall rating: ★ ★ ★			
Classification: Arts		**Readability:**	★ ★ ★
Updating: Monthly		**Content:**	★ ★ ★ ★
Navigation: ★ ★ ★ ★ ★		**Speed:**	★ ★ ★ ★

NL

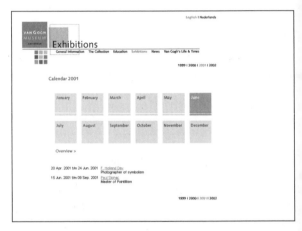

Patterns of bright cubed images mark the homepage of this museum. These flow to sections describing Van Gogh's life, the collection, exhibitions, and a special exhibition entitled Light. The look of the site is bright and airy, summoning a feeling of the summer light that Van Gogh was so adept at creating. Van Gogh's life and techniques are described in fascinating detail over several pages. External concepts and influences receive separate treatments (accessible by clicking on their images), so we find discussions of the Dutch Reformed Church or Cubism. Thus within the analysis of his life, there is a history of Dutch social and art history between 1853 and 1890. Within the collection section, all of Van Gogh's works receive descriptions. The image quality is high, and you won't be driven to distraction waiting for the pictures to expand. The coverage of other artists within the museum doesn't match that of Van Gogh, though seven works make their way onto the website to help explain the background to Van Gogh's work.

Following the link from the homepage to the Light exhibition produces a stimulating analysis of the changing role of light in society and art from 1750 to 1900. Quick and easy to navigate, with attractive and pertinent images, this treatment forms a valuable addition to the site. The essay has been designed as an introduction to an upcoming exhibition and it is hoped that future exhibitions will receive a similar level of online support.

The museum has a regular programme of special exhibitions, details of which appear on the site. The detail should be fuller but the schedule does at least run ahead for two years. The visitor information describes with great care procedures for bringing groups and encouraging potential visitors to email requests for information.

No figures are available for the number of visitors to this website but, given Van Gogh's popularity and the fact that it also appears in Japanese, that figure has got to be high. If you can't make it to Amsterdam, the images here are the next best thing.

www.burtonartgallery.co.uk
Burton Art Gallery and Museum, Bideford

Overall rating: ★ ★ ★ ★			
Classification:	Arts	Readability:	★ ★ ★
Updating:	Unclear	Content:	★ ★ ★
Navigation:	★ ★ ★ ★	Speed:	★ ★ ★

UK

The Burton Art Gallery was originally opened in 1951 by Thomas Burton, a wealthy local businessman, and Hubert Coop, a successful watercolour painter. The intention was to commemorate the untimely death of Burton's daughter, Mary, with a gallery designed to be 'a peaceful haven where one may take a quiet look at beautiful things'. It now boasts three exhibition spaces – hosting both permanent and visiting exhibitions – along with a museum, craft gallery, shop, workshop, lecture theatre and a coffee shop.

Fittingly, then, from its delicate yellow text to its charming rural scenes, the website has a homespun feel that is perfectly in tune with its subject. Moving to the collection through the Gallery link on the homepage, follow the links at the top of the screen to see and read about pictures from the collection. Navigate using the cursor arrows at the top of the screen. A world of pastoral idylls unfolds with each click of the button, the permanent exhibitions featuring works by Coop himself, Sir John Lavery, E Aubrey Hunt and Sir George Clausen. The artist's lives and works are described fully, with an obvious love of the subject. Though nowhere near the scale of many of the sites we've reviewed, for the delicacy with which it treats its subject, this site merits inclusion on any list of the best of the web.

Simply designed and realised, and wonderfully in keeping with its pastoral themes.

www.musee-orsay.fr
Musée d'Orsay

Overall rating: ★ ★ ★ ★			
Classification:	Arts	Readability:	★ ★ ★
Updating:	Irregular	Content:	★ ★ ★
Navigation:	★ ★ ★ ★	Speed:	★ ★ ★ ★

FR

An eye-catching homepage in bright oranges and reds serves as an introduction to one of the triumvirate of world-class museums in Paris. The speed and image quality is high throughout the site. Navigation is good but you'd be well-advised to ignore the advice offered by the Orsay's web designers, helpfully entitled Finding Your Way In This Site – it serves only to confuse. The histories of the building and the collection are described fulsomely. In particular, the rather tortuous collecting policy of the museum and its rivals receives much analysis. Specific areas within the collections are then discussed by type (painting versus sculpture).

The text is full of 'in this gallery we see'; this would be a perfectly sensible way of proceeding if it were accompanied by a plan of the museum on the same page. That way, potential visitors could plan a trip around what is a large space, based on the works and styles that they want to see. One slight disappointment is the lack of any views of the building's interior; it really is the most marvellous, cavernous space and, although the history of the site and the building is outlined, more could be made of a building that rivals the Pyramide and the Pompidou centre as one of the finest display spaces in Paris.

The Programmes section is very full and useful. Selecting any of the options on the left-hand side or at the bottom of the screen produces reams of information on future tours, film programmes, conferences and the like. Some of this information is only available on the French version of the site, but browsers will be redirected automatically. If you have trouble reading the details in French then chances are you wouldn't get much out of the event anyway.

SPECIAL FEATURES

The Musée d'Orsay enjoys a most splendid online shop; the pages look good with their background of weathered gold and titles in bold blues and blacks. The catalogue includes the usual selection of museum shop books, catalogues, guides, clothing and, in that awful word, collectables. The book covers are all illustrated and, although the titles are given in French (even where available in translation), the books have good descriptions in English. Prices are quoted in francs and dollars.

Anyone interested in largely French art (but not architecture) between 1848 and 1914 will find much to see, and more probably, buy here.

www.mmkslw.or.at
Museum of Modern Art

Overall rating: ★ ★ ★ ★

Classification:	Arts	Readability:	★ ★ ★
Updating:	Regularly	Content:	★ ★ ★ ★
Navigation:	★ ★	Speed:	★ ★ ★ ★

Ⓖ

Easily one of the best sites to be found in Austria or Germany. It is often embarrassing how well Germans speak English, given the indifference with which foreign languages are treated by English speakers. Nevertheless, it can be said without fear of rebuke that German museums have made little effort to reach out to an English-speaking audience. However, this boldly designed site has embraced English as the lingua franca of the internet.

The collection consists entirely of 20th-century art and design, featuring works by all the big names – Klee, Pollock, Picasso and so on. Follow the link to the online gallery and you can scroll through selected highlights of the collection. Unfortunately, these are not currently searchable, so a lot of clicking on the Next button is required. Images of the objects appear as thumbnails, and when clicked on expand into a larger window including a text description and analysis of the object. There seem to be 50 or so objects described.

Navigation is via a series of links at the bottom right-hand corner of the title pages. Click the Menu link to bring up the list of options. Some of these are only available in German, but the Archive section, available in English, is the one worth pursuing. You'll find photographs and descriptions of all the objects from the temporary or special exhibitions going back to 1994. The format is the same as that for the online Gallery section devoted to the permanent collections.

SPECIAL FEATURES

The New Museumsquartier The fashion to cover over artistic collections and buildings, thereby creating supra-museums with shops and restaurants all under one roof, has been followed by the Viennese Museum authorities. Follow the link, via Menu and General Information, to view an account of a project to rival the British Museum's Great Court Project, the Louvre's Pyramid or the Libeskin Building at the Victoria & Albert Museum. Using QuickPlayer Tours, extensive text and lots of three-dimensional modelling, this area explains how they intend to physically link the currently diffuse museums of Contemporary Architecture, Children's Life, Folk History and Art and the Leopold Museum with the museum for Contemporary Life. It all sounds impressive, but check out the webcam which covers the scene on the building site. Despite several visits, we could never see anyone doing any work!

Impressive coverage of the collection but perhaps the site is a little too linear – it could do with more interactivity.

www.royalacademy.org.uk
The Royal Academy

Overall rating: ★ ★ ★ ★			
Classification:	Arts	**Readability:**	★ ★ ★
Updating:	Monthly	**Content:**	★ ★
Navigation:	★ ★	**Speed:**	★ ★ ★ ★

UK

The Royal Academy website successfully dispels any notions you may have had of the Royal Academy being a rather stuffy institution, through a slick design in red and black, and a concise writing style that manages to convey the nature of the works on display, without being either too populist in tone or too academic.

The Royal Academy is most well-known for its temporary exhibitions, which are of consistently international class. Recent highlights have included the Monet, Art in the Garden, and the Sensation exhibitions. Coverage of individual exhibitions is variable but, mostly, there are plentiful images from the displays and intelligent analysis of the subject matter. Unfortunately, none of the exhibitions held prior to late 1999 have been given the web treatment, so the most celebrated one currently described is the Van Dyck exhibition of summer 2000.

SPECIAL FEATURES

What's New at the RA lists the latest exhibitions in Exhibitions Diary. There are also links to more detailed descriptions of current exhibitions, which come complete with a biography of the artist. A history of the collections places the paintings in the context of their time, and highlights their contemporary significance. A small selection of illustrations is available, again accompanied by a brief history, as well as details of associated lectures and events.

RA shop provides catalogue details for the Academy's regular exhibitions, illustrates part of the range of gifts inspired by current exhibitions, and also the gift range designed by the Royal Academians.

OTHER FEATURES

Special Features provides contact details, an outline of the Royal Academians, a lecture diary in Public Programme, and tells you how you can Become A Friend.

The Collection provides an opportunity to submit your email details, so that you can receive notification as soon as the RA collection is online.

RA School introduces the Royal Academy as an institute of learning, for prospective artists.

A revolving programme of special exhibitions, including many of the international blockbuster exhibitions, makes this site compulsory for anyone planning a visit to London.

www.tate.org.uk/modern/default.htm
Tate Modern

Overall rating: ★ ★ ★ ★			
Classification:	Arts	**Readability:**	★ ★ ★ ★
Updating:	Regular	**Content:**	★ ★ ★
Navigation:	★ ★	**Speed:**	★ ★ ★

UK

The format and style of the Tate Modern site is similar to that of its mother institution, the Tate Britain (see p.19), and favours simplicity of design, combined with ease of use. Links to all the relevant sections are encapsulated in the menu on the right. You can also access all the websites for the Tate's regional galleries in Liverpool and St Ives, via this menu.

The online catalogue works the same way as that of the Tate Britain site, and is no less impressive in its depth.

SPECIAL FEATURES

Collection Displays The galleries were all designed along the same thematic lines as used for some of those at Tate Britain, so general themes break down into rooms devoted to specific images or ideas. Given the often confusing and diverse nature of modern art, the thematic guides are especially useful here. Themes such as History/Memory/Society and Nude/Action/History take you through a variety of different rooms that may cover the works of an individual artist or a wider issue from within the wider concept under discussion. One quibble: the images within this section could be larger.

The Building is in many ways the most important feature of Tate Modern, and the designers recognise this by including lots of interior views and devoting a section to the architectural and design transformation of the building. This area could benefit from some graphics or plans of the development (such as those found on the Viennese Museum of Modern Art site) but there is a Facts and Figures section that indicates the scale of the project. Details of the extensive shopping and eating facilities within the Museum complex, as well as useful maps and tube information, can all be found in the Visiting Information section.

Special Exhibitions is a timetable of all the temporary exhibitions, which bring art from all over the world to the Tate Gallery. Clicking on the small 'i' icon will reveal more background information on the exhibitons, which often introduce lesser-known artists, as well as established individuals.

Public Programmes lists the forthcoming programme of talks, courses, film conferences and symposia by writers, critics, artists and academics.

Of the same cloth as the main Tate site but with many details of its new and monumental building.

www.uffizi.firenze.it
Uffizi Gallery

Overall rating: ★ ★ ★ ★			
Classification:	Arts	**Readability:**	★ ★ ★
Updating:	Unclear	**Content:**	★ ★ ★
Navigation:	★ ★	**Speed:**	★ ★ ★ ★

IT

Don't be put off by the somewhat garish yellow that confronts you at this site; beneath this unprepossessing façade lies the most superlative display of Italian Renaissance painting in the world. Beyond the paintings, the gallery has been created within the Uffizi palace of the Medici, which is described in painstaking detail on the site. The wealth of history of the palace makes these descriptions fascinating reading. The interior and exterior shots of the building have their work cut out trying to do justice to this marvellous complex of buildings. The descriptions and histories of, among others, the Medici theatre and the church of San Pier Scheraggio are so fascinating that even more images could be used. QuickTime tours are used to great effect in the various gallery spaces, bringing out the sumptuous details within the palace. Within this luxurious atmosphere the individual paintings are displayed to great advantage.

SPECIAL FEATURES

The Gallery Follow the Gallery link from the homepage to open either the index of artists or the alphabetical list. You can find artists by name or school; just scroll down the screen. Slightly confusingly, some of the minor artists only appear under the details of their school rather than their own names. Still, many of the paintings and sculptures are illustrated, with all the images expanding into a full window. We would recommend visiting the Uffizi to experience the

History outlines the story of the Uffizi palace since 1560, when Duke Cosimo De Medici built offices for the magistrates of Florence.

Buildings would not appear at first to be a particularly enticing option, but is a fascinating read. It expands upon the details within the History section, and reveals the Uffizi palace as a centre of Florentine Renaissance history, instead of merely an old building that houses paintings.

News is of interest to the committed art lover and outlines forthcoming attractions plus details of recent restorations, web projects and latest acquisitions.

Experience a superb collection through virtual tours and detailed analysis; it's almost as good as going to the museum itself.

collection first hand, but this enormous gallery of images represents a genuine alternative if you want to understand the breadth of Renaissance art.

Information houses the mundane but necessary information on opening hours, reservations, tours and ticket prices. However, hidden amongst this is a jewel of a section offering QuickTime Virtual Reality tours through an almost unnoticable link. Scroll down the page till you reach the section titled The Gallery, then open the link by clicking on the word 'Second' (underlined, and typed in blue). The tours are relatively quick to download and cover about a quarter of the gallery space. They create a deep impression of the wealth of the collection, travelling through rooms which overflow with the cream of Renaissance art. Browsers get a real sense of the museum and its collections here. The Gallery described above complements the more impressionistic approach of the QuickTime tours very well, allowing surfers to thoroughly immerse themselves in this superb museum and collection.

OTHER SITES OF INTEREST

Rodin Museum, Paris
www.musee-rodin.fr/

Currently very fashionable, Rodin's website describes the sculptures, paintings, collecting, press cuttings and other aspects of his prodigious energies. All of these are fully illustrated and captioned. For those wishing to take some of this experience away with them, there is an online boutique which sells catalogues, reproductions, electronic guides and even T-shirts, all inspired by Rodin. Prices are quoted in Euros and French francs, for anyone wishing to support the Rodin heritage industry.

Sir John Soane's Museum, UK
www.soane.org/

Sir John Soane was a Victorian architect with a mania for collecting. Classical pieces, paintings, architectural views, libraries and ancient Egyptian works can all be found within this charismatic museum in the centre of London. The site is full of information concerning the work of the collections and the curators, who are involved in (for a relatively small museum) a staggering amount of partnerships and international programs. There could be more images here, but the quality of the collections and the uniqueness of Soane's vision shine through this site. Anyone planning a visit to the more well-known London museums should take the time to be enchanted by this small and unique museum.

Hayward Gallery, London
www.hayward-gallery.org.uk

The prestigious South Bank gallery's website offers plenty of background information on contemporary art, including recent purchases for the Arts Council Collection. among these the spotlights on artists such as Gillian Wearing, Terry Frost, Anthony Gormley are worth seeking out. Details of the Hayward's exhibitions and educational activities are given as well as National Touring Exhibitions.

Serpentine Gallery, London
www.serpentinegallery.org

Details of future and current exhibitions are worth referring to, but the Serpentine Gallery Limited Editions are one of the highlights of this site: accessibly priced original editions by leading contemporary artists and photographers are sold online to raise money for the Serpentine's exhibition and education policy.

The Institute of Contemporary Arts (ICA)
www.ica.org.uk

The online offering from the ICA reflects the institute's interest in all media. Check it out to keep up with the cutting edge. (see also p.59)

---

want to read **more reviews** on this subject?

log on to

www.thegoodwebguide.co.uk

Chapter 04

decorative and contemporary art

Any attempt to distinguish between different types of 'art' museum will tend to founder when faced with the breadth and variety of collections possessed by the world's best museums. The Rijksmuseum is best known for its collection of Rembrandts but it also has a substantial holding of medieval sculpture; likewise, the Museum of Fine Arts in Boston possesses fine Classical sculpture but also medieval plates. Decorative art is not a fixed term but rather a generic one for arts and objects that, while being important and beautiful stylistically, are not really fine art. The objects in these collections tend to have a purpose beyond that of mere depiction.

www.si.edu/ndm/
The Cooper Hewitt Design Museum

Overall rating: ★ ★ ★ ★			
Classification:	Arts museum	**Readability:**	★ ★ ★
Updating:	Regular	**Content:**	★ ★ ★
Navigation:	★ ★	**Speed:**	★ ★ ★

US

A bright and attractive homepage greets visitors to this site, who should then follow the links at the top of the page to move around it. Follow the Collections link to read the explanations of what's at the museum. Included in this section are a series of thematic essays describing concepts like applied arts and industrial design.

SPECIAL FEATURES

Design Museum Shop The shop has a superb selection of handbags and bowls, as well as the usual books and catalogues. However, while much of the product is attractively portrayed in the online catalogue, not all of it can be purchased online. This is a pity, given that the shop has recently had a face lift.

The Opulent Eye of Alexander Girard Clicking on the purple and red screen on the left-hand side of the homepage produces an account of Girard's life and work (emphatically not the Girard of 19th-century portraiture fame). This 1960s design icon is represented by all the materials through which he shaped material culture. His textiles, homeware and house designs are explored in this exhibition, which includes photos of Girard's colourful designs and the man himself. A good taster for the exhibition.

Featured Object Unlike some similar features at other museums, these objects really are changed every month.

What's more, they're also analysed in sufficient depth to justify their status as an object of the month. The object at the time of review was a jewel cabinet given by Charles of France to Francis I, King of the Two Sicilies, in 1830. The description of it has eight photographs taken from different angles, including detail shots to illustrate specific examples of craftsmanship.

Ultra-chic and stylish, like most of the collection.

www.mmfa.qc.ca/a-sommaire.html
Montreal Museum of Fine Arts

Overall rating: ★ ★ ★ ★			
Classification:	Arts museum	Readability:	★ ★ ★
Updating:	Regular	Content:	★ ★ ★
Navigation:	★ ★ ★	Speed:	★ ★ ★

(CAN)

It is clear from the homepage that this museum boasts an active and well-designed site. Images from the permanent and temporary collections wink at the viewer from the top of the screen, while the homepage is strewn with links and options. The only danger is that a visitor might miss something of interest. All the temporary exhibitions and many of the permanent collections have a web presence. For their current blockbuster exhibition of works from the Musée de l'Orangerie, featuring Renoir and Picasso, there is a fully fledged virtual tour. Previous temporary exhibitions and the permanent galleries have miniature catalogues of their featured objects. Many of these areas also contain links to relevant web resources, so Asterix fans not sated by the exhibition can gorge themselves on the official Asterix website. The Asterix connection is used to stimulate interest in the classical holdings of the museum, but it also underlines the variety of interests represented within: Renoir and Picasso contrasted with Asterix and Tintin.

The museum's 'cyber boutique' (online store to you and me) is currently under production but will be selling a selection of the usual high-quality museum fare: reproductions and heavyweight books.

SPECIAL FEATURES

Gallery 67 The name of this virtual gallery derives from it complementing the 66 physical galleries. The title is the only sensible part of the endeavour, however. Instead of having objects from the collection, picture essays or even QuickTime tours, this gallery merely contains lots of animated GIFs. Most or all of them seem to have been taken from exhibitions elsewhere on the website. Visitors can live again the triumph that was the revolving 'P' in the homepage for the Picasso exhibition or the introductory icon to the Magritte exhibition. The only use we could find for these images was to download them to use in presentations. We hope there was a point to this exercise; the rest of the site is so fine that we assume there must have been and that it is our fault that we can't see it.

Lots to see and learn but an amazingly obtuse range of special exhibitions means you have to prepare to be surprised and, possibly, disappointed if your interest doesn't feature.

Though perhaps not as well-known as it should be, this museum has an outstanding collection that covers art history from Ancient Egypt to the 19th century, including Islamic and Asian departments. The site itself is compact, so navigation is easy and the download speed is fast. Image quality is high but, with the exception of the Archimedes Exhibition, there is no interactivity. Ten or so highlights are chosen from each department to represent the collection. These are given brief descriptions and analyses. The images can be magnified without any slip in their quality. The number of items chosen means that you can develop a proper sense of the quality of the collection beyond only one or two stars. Future exhibitions are not covered to the same extent but all the obvious information is there.

If you're planning a visit, be sure to check the calendar of events because there are lectures and tours everyday. The museum has a shop but there is no online store.

SPECIAL FEATURES

Archimedes Palimpsest This online exhibition, accessed via the Permanent Collection link on the homepage, describes the life and works of Archimedes. By following the timeline along the bottom of the screen, browsers can find out details about specific events in Archimedes's life and times. More general information about the manuscript and its history can be found by scrolling over the icons at the top of the page. The stimulus for this exhibition was the purchase of a palimpsest (by a private collector for £2 million) featuring the earliest known copy of Archimedes's work. We should not get too excited; it still dates from 1,300 years after he died. The history of the manuscript and the definition of a palimpsest (a manuscript that has been reused on which some of the original text survives) are all fully elucidated for those who are interested.

Full of information about America's best collection – outside the Met – of Classical and Medieval Art.

www.mfa.org
Museum of Fine Arts, Boston

Overall rating: ★ ★ ★			
Classification: Arts		**Readability:**	★ ★ ★ ★
Updating: Irregular		**Content:**	★ ★ ★
Navigation: ★ ★ ★		**Speed:**	★ ★ ★

US 🔒

Speed seems to be the crucial issue with this site; the quality of the information, images and links is high but you won't know unless you're prepared to wait. Of course, all servers could be quicker but, for a site of this size and importance, they should probably spend the money. A quick tip if you're surfing from outside the US: log on first thing in the morning, before America wakes up, and you will find a notable increase in speed on some American sites.

The collections section has accounts of the various departments holdings but there doesn't seem to be any great scheme to the layout. There is also an account of the museum's steps to prove provenance for paintings acquired during and after the Second World War in this section. Some improvement in structure would seem in order, although the navigation buttons and links all work well. Not that this is much use: if the site has little internal logic, efficient links won't help.

The search facility (accessible at the bottom of the homepage) works well but also illustrates the patchiness of coverage of the collections; there is plenty about some and very little about others. The exhibitions section has a thorough account of all the previous and upcoming exhibitions. Accounts and images for previously held exhibitions go back to a Winslow Homer exposition in 1996. It is difficult to demonstrate the scope of their previous and upcoming exhibitions. Among many others, note the divergences between exhibitions on Thracian Jewellery, Chinese prints from the 19th century and the paintings of Monet and John Singer Sargent. Of course, not all the exhibitions receive a similar level of treatment on the web but all have at least some images and a basic overview of the themes. Intriguingly, they also have a link straight to the catalogue for the exhibition in their online shop that is second to none (see below). In a similar vein, the museum offers an email service with news of the latest exhibitions and new product in the shop.

SPECIAL FEATURES

Online Shop Despite being rather slow, the museum's online store is one of the best among the US museum sites. It's not as large as the Metropolitan's shop but the products are of high quality and the store site works well. Almost all the products are illustrated (with many images expandable) and given satisfying descriptions. The shop is updated seasonally and has a section for merchandise connected to particular exhibitions. Uniquely, to our knowledge, the site offers a gift-wrapping service which, considering the nature of many of the products and their cost, seems to be an extremely useful, not to say compulsory service. If you're spending £200 dollars on a cocktail shaker for a friend, you're going to want it nicely wrapped.

One-hour tour This feature picks 13 of the most outstanding items from the collections. They are well illustrated and can also be picked out from the map of the museums. The object descriptions are detailed but could perhaps be longer. Still, the tour does provide a very good introduction to the breadth of an extensive collection.

Explore Ancient Egypt Through a cunning use of images, film clips and sound, the designers have created an award-winning area covering the extensive (40,000 objects), permanent Egyptian Collection. The approach is that usually adopted by Egyptian galleries, with sections on mummies, daily life and the like. Each section is introduced by a video clip (RealPlayer) of a curator introducing the theme, usually with reference to a specific item in the collection. The video footage is pretty grainy but the obvious enthusiasm of the curators shines through.

An attractive site with a wide coverage of artists, periods and styles but, frustratingly, random coverage of their own collections. Still, the shop alone makes it worth a visit.

www.khm.at/
The Vienna Kunst Historisches Museum

Overall rating: ★ ★ ★

Classification:	Arts museum	Readability:	★ ★ ★ ★
Updating:	Regular	Content:	★ ★ ★
Navigation:	★ ★ ★	Speed:	★ ★

AU

Austria's National Museum has one of the world's most spectacular collections. The collection varies from Classical Egypt to 17th-century Baroque. The site appears in both English and German and has a simple, elegant layout, with links that work smoothly and quickly (though note the comments below on the Exhibitions section). Overviews are provided of each department's holdings, with many of the pieces illustrated and described. The images are of good quality and, although not expandable, sufficient size. The introductions and the object descriptions could be longer and more detailed, but they do provide a good idea of the breadth of the collection. This is particularly important for the Egyptian and Classical galleries, both of which are closed for renovation.

The special Exhibitions section contains much detail about their subjects. One thing to note is that you must click on the text title, not the image to load the pages. The most recent exhibition covers the artistic patronage of Francis I. Press releases, details of television coverage, lectures, concerts and tours all supplement the copious art historical information. Following an account of the historical and artistic background to Francis's reign, his patronage is analysed and his favourite artists and their pieces are described and illustrated. Not all the future special exhibitions receive quite so much coverage but this is not wholly surprising, given their range.

The Museum section contains all the standard visiting information, opening times, buses, cafés and the like. Unfortunately, it does not make clear which galleries are open when and what exactly will be being restored or renovated at a particular time. Past visits to the museum in Vienna have been somewhat spoilt by the number of galleries closed for renovation, but that is partly the curse of a large collection and gallery space.

SPECIAL FEATURES

Online Store What is described as the online store seems in fact to be a catalogue from which orders can be emailed. Prices are quoted in schillings and euros but there are no details of payment or delivery beyond that. It is possible that they will appear in the areas that 'are under construction'. Despite this, the shop is well stocked with tasteful products derived from the collections. Postcards, books, replicas, jewellery, scarves, CD-ROMS and videos are all available via an online booking form. The products derived from the Classical holdings are as good as – if not better than – those offered by the British Museum. The other notable products are the series of games and puzzles in the Learn about Art through Playing section. They look stimulating, even if they're the kind of thing that parents will become more involved in than their children.

Perhaps this museum is not as well known as it should be, given the quality of the collection; hopefully, this competent site will boost its profile.

www.vmfa.state.va.us/
Virginia Museum of Fine Arts

Overall rating: ★ ★ ★			
Classification:	Arts museum	**Readability:**	★ ★ ★ ★
Updating:	Monthly	**Content:**	★ ★ ★
Navigation:	★ ★	**Speed:**	★ ★

US

Be careful not to click on any of the images on the homepage, as you will be immediately presented with the copyright details for the images. Avoiding this and remembering to scroll down the homepage, rather than looking for a link to follow, you'll be confronted with lots of news and gallery links. Some of the objects have their own catalogue-style entries containing descriptions and attempts to place the objects within their wider context. These are laudable aims but it is a pity that the objects described cover only a fraction of the collection. For example, the Ancient Mediterranean has only two objects, one of which is repeated in the African section (it's an Egyptian statue).

The temporary and forthcoming exhibitions are fully described and well illustrated, although few of the individual objects are described in any detail. The range of these special exhibitions is broad, exciting and international, with Fabergé, Modern Sculpture and John Singer Sargent all featuring in recent examples. Tickets for the special exhibitions can be ordered online, using a system that seems to work for all the visitor attractions in Virginia. The museum seems to profit greatly from its relations within the state and is full of links to other museums, galleries and institutions in Virginia. This can be most obviously seen in the Japanese heritage project Two Views of Kabuki.

The shop's products are described in rather general terms, and there is no real online catalogue or ordering. Instead, products can be ordered using a fax and a downloadable (PDF) form. There is, however, a wide range of books, each of which is well described and reviewed.

SPECIAL FEATURES

Two Views of Kabuki Having an illustrated account of the Kabuki style of Japanese theatre as a core, this part of the site acts as a homepage for the study of Japanese art. It provides copious details for teachers, all stringently pegged against Virginia state's educational stages, along with complete course notes that detail websites, videos and downloads which teachers can use to elaborate on themes within the course.

Virginia is well served by its museum and its commitment to online learning.

OTHER SITES OF INTEREST

Danish National Museum
www.smk.dk/
Smooth and chic, this site has some pleasing images which are let down only by their small size. The collection and range of exhibitions is large and of high quality at the Danish National Museum, but very little of it is accessible from this website. The bookshop looks to be well stocked (at least they say it is) but there is no online shop – so you will have to go and look for yourself.

The Fan Museum, UK
www.fan-museum.org/
Though perhaps not to everyone's taste, this museum has a truly unique collection that is made much of on this site. Documenting the history of fans from the ancient world through to the 19th century, the site enthuses about its rather narrow subject through images, diagrams and special exhibitions. There is a small online catalogue of books and exhibition catalogues (there are new exhibitions every three months) which can be ordered over the phone. For those willing to spend a bit more money, there are also details of the entertaining and banqueting facilities that are available for hire with the Orangery.

Geffrye Museum, UK
www.geffrye-museum.org.uk/
This charming site has a rather homely feel, which is apposite given that the museum is dedicated to English domestic interiors from the 16th century to the present day. Though somewhat slim, the site does have some images of this lively museum, while the historical approach is complemented by a vivacious and upbeat series of programs and workshops. At the time of review, they were running Groovy 60s programs, allowing visitors to decorate cups and plates as well as make jewellery. These programs are explained on the site, along with the more prosaic information about location and opening hours.

Ian Potter Museum of Art, Australia
www.art-museum.unimelb.edu.au/

A very sophisticated homepage of orange and black, reminiscent of Athenian vases. Hosted as part of the University of Melbourne, this museum has the largest collection of antipodean pottery in the world. This modernism is complemented by small classical and medieval collections, all of which can be searched using an online database that contains brief descriptions and sometimes images of the collection. For anyone able to get to Australia, the museum runs an enormous number of study programs and lectures. Again, these are mainly on the works of modern potters.

Institute of Contemporary Arts, UK
www.ica.org.uk

Not surprisingly, one of the niftiest spaces in which to see new, innovative art – not forgetting film, theatre, gigs, club nights and all the rest – in London, also boasts the swishiest website. Decked out in simple blacks and whites, it gives you everything you'll need to know about joining or visiting the ICA, boozing and eating in the way cool bar and café, taking advantage of their excellent education workshops, or even just browsing the various guides to post-modernity in the bookshop. As for the website itself, click on the box marked newmediacentre.com and you'll find youself waving bye-bye to those pipes and fishes you used to call a screensaver. Why not treat your desktop to one of Squid Soup's soothingly minimalist, multi-user sound-and-vision packages? Alternatively, there's plenty of online art experimentation to admire, be it the extensions of Squid Soup's Alt Zero sound installations, the DARE (Digital Arts Research and Experimentation) project, or the worryingly compulsive Sodaconstructor (a rolling, interactive spring device that this reviewer spent far too much time playing with). There's also a host of other links to various cyber-galleries and cyber-artists, all of them fascinating. There's plenty of scope for more online material here, but with

Stencilmakers (Urban Guerrilla Artists) under construction, more Squid Soup material on the way, and DARE just in its infancy, it's clear that the ICA is setting one swanky standard for online art.

Museum of Costume
www.museumofcostume.co.uk/

This rare collection of historic costume is worth a visit for probably the most esoteric online catalogue in the world. Alongside images of clothes from the museum, there is also a searchable database of English waistcoats from the 18th century. A minority interest, maybe, but the catalogue works efficiently, as does the rest of the navigation and design of the site. The only problem that we found was the poor speed of the image download.

The Mackintosh House
www.hunterian.gla.ac.uk/MacHouse

An excellent online tour of the Charles Rennie Mackintosh house lovingly details the reconstruction of the principal interriors from the Glasgow home of the famed Scottish architect and designer, and his artist wife Margaret Macdonald Mackintosh. This is part of the Hunterian Museum's website, reviewed on p.79.

The Crafts Council Online
www.craftscouncil.org.uk

The paucity of pictures on the site means that the pages are very quick to load. Coming soon is a searchable calendar of UK crafts events. Currently, you will find exhibition details and numerous, downloadable documents including teachers notes, a national guide to the craft shops and galleries of Britain.

palaces, cathedrals and ruins

Although all the museums and galleries that we have looked at so far are designed to be visited, here we turn to those institutions that are more concerned with a sense of place than with their collections. While the Palace of the Louvre is an inspiring building, millions would flock to see the collections pretty much wherever they were displayed; but it is nicer to see them in a palace. Althorp House, the childhood home of Diana, Princess of Wales, was only opened to the public after her death, and the crowds that flock there go more to catch a sense of her than to view an 18th-century manor house. Similarly, while Stonehenge is a very evocative site that attracts lots of people with leanings toward the New Age (a fact well-documented on their website), far fewer visitors go to Avebury (a similar site to Stonehenge) – despite the fact that it is much bigger and generally more impressive. Rather than the place or site, it is the ideas associated with it that tend to matter.

The choices for this section quite markedly reflect a bias towards England. Again, this is largely due to the lack of English language content on sites originating outside the UK or the US. It also reflects the preponderance of historical houses and sites within the UK. American Museums tend to possess fabulous websites, but as a whole the country is not that well known for its country houses or charming Stone Age ruins (Agecroft in Richmond, Virginia excepted).

www.chateauversailles.fr
Palace of Versailles

Overall rating: ★ ★ ★ ★			
Classification:	Palace	**Readability:**	★ ★ ★
Updating:	Unclear	**Content:**	★ ★ ★
Navigation:	★ ★ ★	**Speed:**	★ ★ ★ ★

(FR)

The Palace of Versailles, created by Louis XIV, revels in a splendid site. Music greets your entrance to the homepage, while options and links flood the screen. By using a sketch of the house rather than a memory hungry photograph, the screen downloads instantly with a display advertising their adopt-a-tree scheme (following a large storm in 1999). Further options appear all over the page, and, if one were being critical, the positioning is a trifle haphazard. Having said that, the links do lead to some fascinating areas to explore. There are maps and details of the extensive range of different tours and activities. Sections of the instrument, furniture, pictures and porcelain collections can be sampled, along with high-quality images and illuminating descriptions. The images can be zoomed in quite easily and speedily (David's Napoleon and his Eagles disappeared into pixels in a mere three clicks). These collections are complemented by an object of the month/season section. At the time of review, this was displaying a fabulous Riesner, a desk used by Marie Antoinette which was recently brought at auction by Versailles.

There are so many links throughout the site that it can take quite a while to get your bearings; like the house itself, the site is full of surprises and twists. Examples include potted biographies of figures connected to the palace, from Louis XIV to Charles de Gaulle, as well as anecdotes and a facts and figures section (the scale of the house can be ascertained from the fact that there are over 150 different varieties of peach and apple trees in the gardens). For such a major site, it is surprising to find no online shop or even a catalogue and an email form. Similarly, there seems to have been no attempt to involve children in any way. Bar a game of Skill and a treasure hunt, both held in the garden, children do not appear on the site at all.

SPECIAL FEATURES
The 360-degree views of the Great Courtyard, the Hall of Mirrors and the King's Chamber are very impressive. The viewer is fixed on one spot and the panorama slowly rolls around; the sensation is like turning slowly on the spot. While the viewer lacks the ability to zoom in or change perspective, the rolling round of the majestic courtyard and the lavish hall of mirrors works well, giving an effective sense of scale and grandeur. Due to its relative simplicity, the feature doesn't take long to download. Because of this and the maintenance of a higher picture quality, it's much more effective than the more complex and ultimately unsatisfactory QuickTime tours found at other sites.

Insouciant and unconcerned with a shop or inconveniences like children, but good coverage of a superb collection and buildings.

www.Schoenbrunn.at

Schönbrunn Palace

Overall rating: ★ ★ ★ ★			
Classification:	Palace	Readability:	★ ★
Updating:	Unclear	Content:	★ ★ ★
Navigation:	★ ★ ★ ★	Speed:	★ ★ ★ ★ ★

(AU)

The rather sickly yellow that adorns the outside of this 17th-century palace similarly dominates the homepage for the palace of Austria's emperors. Ignore the colour of the house to explore this opulent site, which fully captures the glories of the Hapsburg Empire. Travelling through 32 rooms of the house, surfers can understand the history of this amazing palace through copious images and descriptions, as well as views of the garden and some of the amazing conceits built there.

Since the tour takes the same route as that offered to physical visitors, and much of the information mirrors that found in the guidebook, web browsers are genuinely 'visiting' Schönbrunn. There are accounts of Emperor Franz Joseph entertaining diplomats in the billiard room and having English loos installed in his bedroom. The accounts of the magnificent Gloriette (an enormous triple arch overlooking a fountain) and the large mock ruin of a Carthaginian Temple are similarly prosaic. Many of these rooms – especially the view from the House to the Gloriette – are glorious and perhaps deserve much larger images or even QuickPlayer tours. Still, given the large canvas of the house that the website does such justice to, it would be churlish to make too much of this.

Curiously, there is no online shop or even catalogue. There is an option to purchase up to seven tickets online (payment is on collection), which is handy since one would otherwise have to wait for at least two hours to get a timed slot, which could be painful given Schönbrunn's location in a rather dreary area of Vienna. Beyond the content related to the house there is a list of daily and evening events and happenings within the house and grounds. Schönbrunn boasts its own Orchestra Company and Puppeteers, both of whom perform regularly. The house and the Events section has links to these company's sites, as well as details of the company's histories and their relationship with the house and the Hapsburgs.

It is unusual to find on a site of this kind a section entitled Public Relations Work and Commercial Results. Here, one can find graphs of revenue and visitor numbers which illuminate the true cost of running and maintaining such a property. However, there is some unintentional levity among this seriousness. On how many other museum's websites would one find the phrases: 'net product per member of staff' or 'overall gastronomical concept'?

Does justice to a large, gaudy but sometimes beautiful palace, which must rate as one of the foremost in Europe.

www.sherlock-holmes.co.uk
Sherlock Holmes Museum

Overall rating: ★ ★ ★			
Classification:	Fiction	**Readability:**	★ ★ ★
Updating:	Regularly	**Content:**	★ ★ ★ ★ ★
Navigation:	★ ★ ★ ★	**Speed:**	★ ★

UK

Recently redesigned, this site will appeal to all those who have ever marvelled at the steely logic of the most famous detective in the world. The museum is not at all concerned that Holmes's address of 22b Baker Street doesn't actually exist, and the site displays a similar lack of concern over Holmes's fictional status. Overlooking this minor issue, it is quite a charming site. Like many sites that deal with subjects which tend to excite obsession, it is difficult not to become a bit enamoured of the subject by exposure to other people's enthusiasm. There is a virtual tour of Holmes's study, which seems more garish than the television programmes would have it. You can zoom in and out using the two buttons at the bottom left of the window. Whether Sherlock Holmes's flat might ever have looked like this is a moot point but the effect is still worth a look.

Touring Holmes's sitting room is the highlight of a tour which includes details of other rooms in the house and their related collections of memorabilia and artefacts. Thrill at the sight of Watson's diary or Holmes's slippers, or at a series of miniature waxworks depicting scenes from the novels. Images of some of this esoteric collection have made it on to the site. There is even a chatroom and guest book in which you can leave messages for, and talk online to, fellow devotees of Holmes; you should note that it takes a while to load and you have to give yourself a nickname. Oh, and all the best nicknames have already been taken.

SPECIAL FEATURES

Online Shop If you've ever fancied owning bears dressed like Holmes and Watson, this is the place for you. The online shop has a range of similarly delightful (or horrendous, depending on where you stand) gifts for the Holmes enthusiast who you don't like much. All of the items are illustrated, although the picture download is slow. You can pay by all the internationally accepted credit cards (including Western Union Money Transfer; if you're willing to go to those lengths, though, you should probably seek a more healthy obsession). There is a currency converter, which, apart from being aesthetically hideous, works well. All transactions are held on a secure server, although this isn't as secure as encrypted transactions would be.

Sherlock Holmes Online This has to be one of the few places on the net where you can read the entire Sherlock Holmes oeuvre. Should you choose to, you can read the 250 pages of the Hound of the Baskervilles with illustrations via your screen and mouse. Whether this is good for either your eyes or your local bookshop is not stated, but we feel that most of those interested in the site would have copies of the book already. Still, it is an impressive endeavour.

This site will be a favourite for the Sherlock Holmes aficionado; for the less committed, the option to read Holmes online may save them some money in library fines.

www.stonehenge.co.uk
Stonehenge

Overall rating: ★ ★ ★ ★			
Classification:	Prehistoric	Readability:	★ ★ ★ ★
Updating:	Unclear	Content:	★ ★
Navigation:	★ ★ ★	Speed:	★ ★ ★

UK

This site covers Stonehenge and the comparable sites of Averbury and Barrow. The homepage, set in modern whites and blues, offers a series of links down the left-hand side of the page to a wide range of options. It is refreshingly different from some of the more guidebook-based websites. The text is portentous in the extreme: all three prehistoric areas are described in tones along the lines of 'the oldest', 'the biggest' and 'the most mysterious'.

The sections on the history of each location are usefully illustrated, providing a background for any visitors to the area. They avoid many of the more bizarre theories (which appear in the book shop) but are slightly handicapped by the lack of coherent evidence from the site. The proposed visitor centre at Stonehenge itself will probably help with producing an agreed interpretation of the site, or at least a coherent account of the evidence from the site.

Instead of virtual tours and images of artefacts from the site, any potential tourist is well catered for with lists of local hotels, pubs and the like, including a list of other places of interest. As a side issue, we are curious as to who would decide that they needed to book a wedding photographer when looking for information about Stonehenge. The list of similar options on the site gives it the feel of a business directory.

SPECIAL FEATURES

While the rest of the site could do with more content, the online shop is a marvel, crammed with descriptions and images of products ranging from dowsing kits for beginners to Celtic-inspired jewellery. Ordering is genuinely online (rather than via email) and the level of credit card encryption is satisfactory. If you're looking for that unusual gift for friends who are passionate about crop circles, this would certainly be a useful site to visit.

A little less of the New Age and a bit more of the academic might not go amiss, but this is a useful site for anyone planning to visit or, indeed, get married in the area.

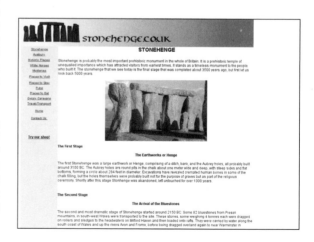

www.tower-of-london.com

Camelot International: Tower of London

Overall rating: ★ ★ ★ ★			
Classification: Castle		**Readability:**	★ ★ ★ ★ ★
Updating: Unknown		**Content:**	★ ★ ★ ★
Navigation: ★ ★ ★ ★ ★		**Speed:**	★ ★ ★

UK

A booming voice blares out from the homepage for this site, followed by portentous music that could drive you to distraction if you don't turn your speakers down. The music combines with voiceovers at various points to good effect; you occasionally have to wait for it to download but, otherwise, the site does run smoothly and relatively quickly. Navigation is straightforward, with the same series of links appearing on the left-hand side of each page.

Within this framework the site is packed with information, presented in an accessible manner. Ghost stories, rumours and interviews are all related, with gusto, through a mix of voiceovers and music. The emphasis is quite firmly on the history of the site and its staff; browsers should note that this is not the official website of the Tower of London but is in effect the website for the staff. This means there are few details about opening times or the history of the castle but lots of the blood-and-guts variety. We have accounts of Guy Fawkes's torture, public execution and the use for three years of the moat as a cesspit. There is also a game based on the premise that the king is going to cut your head off if you don't win an archery contest – well, you can't say we didn't warn you. For online shopping and ticket sales, surfers are directed to the official site.

SPECIAL FEATURES

Interviews The personal feel of the site is maintained through substantial interviews with the Beefeaters; here, they regale the public with tales of their lives (most are ex-servicemen) and their work at the Tower of London. The interview with the Raven Master is particularly charming.

Q.T.V.R. There are QuickTime views of three rooms within the castle complex; tellingly, one of them is the Beefeater's bar, complete with costumes in display cases. These work as well as everywhere else that uses them.

Scrapbook More images of the Beefeaters behind the scenes, as it were, can be found in the excellent scrapbook containing pictures and comments from visitors and staff.

What the Warder Overheard This section contains anecdotes from the warders concerning the naiveties of the general public. Having worked in national museums, I recommend that all visitors read this section before they ask questions of the staff at any museum or gallery.

Virtual Tour This works very well, using a voiceover and still images of the castle. Download is quick and the tour flows responsively as you click through it. The voiceover is given by a Beefeater, and most of the images depict our putative guide showing groups of tourists around the castle. You must click on the icon of the Beefeater at the bottom of the page to continue the tour or the first section will loop and play again. The size of the tour is very impressive, though.

A wonderful site that benefits greatly from the enthusiasm of its staff.

www.winchester-cathedral.org.uk
Winchester Cathedral

Overall rating: ★ ★ ★ ★			
Classification:	Cathedral	Readability:	★ ★ ★ ★
Updating:	Monthly	Content:	★ ★ ★
Navigation:	★ ★ ★ ★ ★	Speed:	★ ★ ★ ★

UK

This site flows easily through sections on the history, the calling, the music and life of this grandiose, medieval church. Navigation is straightforward and the number of frills is low; information (notably the daily events/service sheet) is full but slightly abrupt in tone. Images are reserved for a section called The Gallery, and although this approach keeps the speed of access high, it does lend the site a rather monochromatic aspect. Nevertheless, the images are good quality and expandable, showing architectural views of the exterior and interior as well as more detailed images of some of the objects from the splendid medieval treasury.

SPECIAL FEATURES
Beyond the usual information concerning location, entrance times and the like, the Winchester site has a quite extensive range of musical CDs for sale online. All are recordings of the Cathedral Choir singing a range of music from Christmas Carols to Verdi, and the assortment is wider than that on comparable ecclesiastical sites. Sadly, there are no sound files to download, a technique which is used to great effect on the Westminster Abbey site.

A small but perfectly formed site.

www.yorkminster.org
York Minster Cathedral

Overall rating: ★ ★ ★ ★			
Classification:	Cathedral	Readability:	★ ★ ★ ★
Updating:	Regularly	Content:	★ ★ ★ ★
Navigation:	★ ★ ★	Speed:	★ ★ ★

UK

Easily the best of the European church sites, Yorkminster is positively bursting with material. The artistic and architectural achievements of the interior are fully explored in the online tour; be sure to click on the images (they expand quickly to fill a new window) to appreciate the detail of the stained glass in particular. The history of the Cathedral and, indeed, Christianity in England is explored in the Chronicle section – follow the link at the top of the page. Again, this is well illustrated and the text is long and vigorous, with many names and terms having footnotes. It must be a rare website indeed that can boast a potted biography of King Penda of the sixth century alongside an analysis of the causes and effects of the Reformation.

For those with more secular interests, within the Chapter House link sit full descriptions of the cathedral's range of conference and banqueting facilities. Navigation is generally good, although some of the pages are enormous; be sure to scroll right down to the bottom of the page. There is no shop as yet, though one is promised soon; keep your eyes peeled.

SPECIAL FEATURES

The Online Prayer is a unique feature, via which Christians from all over the world have emailed prayers to the Cathedral. The effect is surprisingly moving (helped by a very simple design), even for an arch member of secular society. For those unlikely ever to visit this wonderful religious space, these online prayers almost capture the sense. Still, the effect might be greater if someone had bothered to check the spelling: we suspect that the Saints 'know' things rather than 'No' them.

Professionally designed and full of insights – but maintains a profoundly spiritual air.

www.althorp-house.co.uk
Althorp House

Overall rating: ★★★★★			
Classification:	Stately home	Readability:	★★★
Updating:	Unclear	Content:	★★★
Navigation:	★★	Speed:	★

UK

Considering that Althorp has only been opened to the public since the death of Diana, Princess of Wales, both the Visitor Centre and its website are very polished and slick. Though perhaps lacking any real depth or subtlety, the site still boasts extensive coverage of the house and, more importantly, Diana. The site runs by opening new windows on every choice, which can be aggravating as some take a while to download. Furthermore, some of the links are rather small and difficult to click on. Nevertheless, for anyone interested in Diana as a person or phenomenon there is much of interest here. Displays about her life, featuring images and dresses, are set against the background of the historic Althorp House. In the media centre, browsers can download images from the displays in a PDF format as well as look at some rather out-of-date press coverage. The Visiting Althorp section is full of pertinent information – especially the advice to wear sensible shoes!

The option to buy tickets online and have them sent to your home address should be very useful for potential visitors. Given that the house is only open for two months a year, and bearing in mind the Princess's international following, visitor demand must be high. The tickets are sold for specific days and their availability is adjusted daily.

With the exception of the bound copies of Earl Spencer's funeral oration, the online shop consists entirely of bone china objects in a variety of finishes. All feature design is inspired by Diana, Althorp or the Spencer Family Crest. It is difficult to see exactly what payment encryption they are using, but the online ticketing system is designed by Globalticketmaster (a large, reputable company); they seem to be secure, so the shop is probably using the same facility for taking credit card payments. Nevertheless, it is worrying that they don't describe what system they are using.

SPECIAL FEATURE

Online Tour Given the limited opening times for Althorp, it seems likely that these virtual tours will prove popular. There are views of the interior and exterior of the house (seven in all) but probably the most popular and effective is that of the burial island. Trees predominate and there are no pictures or details of the kind that QuickTime viewers can blur. The effect is tranquil.

Very sophisticated and stylish; almost so good that people may not make the pilgrimage to the site.

www.hadrians-wall.org
Hadrian's Wall

Overall rating: ★ ★ ★ ★			
Classification:	Archaeology	Readability:	★ ★ ★ ★
Updating:	Unclear	Content:	★ ★ ★ ★
Navigation:	★ ★	Speed:	★ ★ ★

UK

At first glance, this site does not seem to do justice to what is one of the world's most important ancient archaeological sites. The style is slightly pedestrian, with very few images. However, it is a positive encyclopaedia of useful information for anyone planning to visit Hadrian's Wall.

The information tends towards the practical, with copious details of transport routes, accommodation, walking tours, other areas to visit and the like. These all emphasise how historically interesting and rich the area is, encouraging all sorts of different visitors to look beyond the wall. Anyone planning to visit the area could well be better off visiting this site than any of the local tourist offices. Among these details are scattered many links to other relevant websites; where else could you find a link to the UNESCO World Heritage Centre alongside a guide to the Inter-regional Trans-Pennine Railway? In addition, the links section (it also appears in the history section) contains a link to the University of Newcastle classical site, which features an unexpectedly good virtual museum and a QuickPlayer tour of a reconstructed Mithraic Temple.

There could be more about the history and development of the wall during the Roman period, but the designers are hampered – as at Stonehenge – by a lack of evidence. There is plenty of evidence for daily life on the wall but very little about its wider purpose and development. Perhaps greater

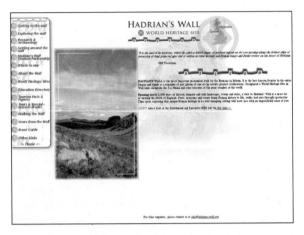

For other enquiries, please contact us at info@hadrians-wall.org

comparison could be made with the border fortresses and walls that were built along the Rhine at the same time. However, this lack of any comparative evidence only serves to underline how unique Hadrian's Wall is. The history of the wall appears instead through biographies of the notable (largely Victorian) scholars who first surveyed and dug it.

There's an amateur feel to this site, but it is packed with practical information and enthusiasm.

www.hrp.org.uk
Historic Royal Palaces

Overall rating: ★ ★ ★			
Classification:	Palaces	Readability:	★ ★
Updating:	Monthly	Content:	★ ★ ★
Navigation:	★ ★ ★	Speed:	★ ★ ★

UK

Covering the historic Royal Palaces of Kew, Hampton Court, Kensington Palace, the Tower of London and the Banqueting House, this site has plenty to offer the prospective visitor to London. On a crisp white background, simply displayed, are a host of expandable images from the Palaces, along with facts, histories and games that are all calculated to encourage the potential visitor.

Though Hampton Court receives more coverage than the other palaces on the site the approach is similar for them all, with timelines, photos and descriptions. The speed is universally good and provided that you always follow the red links on the left of the page the navigation is always good. Anyone wanting to visit England's Royal Palaces who is pushed for time could get a full sense of the grandeur and history of them through exploring the site.

SPECIAL FEATURES

Hampton Court Following the link to Hampton Court, browsers can view images and read commentary on a series of rooms through the house and its recently refurbished Elizabethan Kitchens. The gardens are described as fully. If you follow the link to the left you can explore the history of the house via a timeline; click on any date or period along it and the activity of the time will be described year by year. This chronological approach tends to constrain the narrative to high politics and cultural affairs; so-and-so died, so and so painted his famous whatever. Perhaps a trifle more levity in the choice of historical anecdote might be in order. Still, there is a lot of information here.

Fun and Games This is more lighthearted in tone, and can be found by following the link from the homepage. You're quizzed on your knowledge of the Kings and Queens of England and their palaces. All the answers can be found on the website – beware of getting too many wrong because you might end up with your electronic head cut off !

Wonderful summary of some of Britain's most evocative Royal Sites.

want to read **more reviews** on this subject?

log on to

www.thegoodwebguide.co.uk

www.romanbaths.co.uk
Roman Baths, Bath

Overall rating: ★ ★ ★			
Classification:	Archaeology	Readability:	★ ★ ★ ★
Updating:	Unknown	Content:	★ ★ ★
Navigation:	★ ★ ★	Speed:	★ ★ ★

UK

An attractive range of pastel hues greets the visitor to this homepage, with coloured icons to differentiate between the many options. The navigation is simplicity itself, with links expanding like branches off a tree to an exciting range of options, including the gallery, a virtual tour and film footage. Alongside this are full and more mundane details about the restaurant, opening times and the like.

The gallery section contains images from the site (largely but not exclusively those found in the online tour) which, importantly, are only expandable in this section. Follow the link into the history section to see more of the objects and the history of the complex. Further depth is added to the history of the site by the object of the month selection; at the time of review, this displayed a series of coin finds from Bath. There is a search feature that allows you to jump right to the area of interest within the site, which also includes details of recent archaeological projects within the city and describes the work of the local archaeological unit. The images are all high quality and the site works quickly.

SPECIAL FEATURES

Tour The images could be bigger (they appear in an expanded form in the gallery) but the text is readable and informative, even if the author should make a more careful distinction between the Bath and Temple complexes. The tour takes you through some of the rooms and the notable

www.salisburycathedral.org.uk
Salisbury Cathedral, UK

Overall rating: ★ ★ ★			
Classification:	Cathedral	**Readability:**	★★★★
Updating:	Irregularly	**Content:**	★★
Navigation:	★★★	**Speed:**	★★★★

UK

objects within them, explaining the purpose of the rooms, how they fit into the complex as a whole and any significant objects within them.

Video Tour Using QuickPlayer, the download for this is quick and simple – it takes about a minute on a 56K modem. Once it's complete, classical music accompanies a camera zooming down from the heavens into the complex. The results are impressive if impressionistic, stimulating the viewer to visit the site in person. The camera flies around the site, taking a different route than that of the tour in order to give a sense of the temple/bath complex's scale.

One of the best-preserved classical sites in England is done proud by this atmospheric and detailed site.

The Salisbury Cathedral site is sophisticated in style and operation, with links that move you smoothly and quickly through a plethora of pages. This slickness is characteristic of the corporate feel of the website; it may have gone a trifle too far for a religious site by including a management-speak mission statement on its homepage. Minor quibbles aside, there is a lot of information attractively displayed here, with timelines and biographies describing the history and personalities associated with this monumental building. The history of the Cathedral complex is complemented by an extensive FAQ section, as well as more visitor-minded information like travel links. Unfortunately, according to the FAQs you cannot get married unless you come from the parish – and worryingly, despite the spire being 404ft tall, it only rests on foundations 4ft deep!

A very modern, well-organised site for one of the finest High Medieval Churches in Europe.

www.royal.gov.uk/palaces

Buckingham Palace, Windsor Castle, Holyrood House etc

Overall rating: ★ ★ ★			
Classification: Palaces		**Readability:**	★ ★ ★
Updating: Unclear		**Content:**	★ ★
Navigation: ★ ★ ★		**Speed:**	★ ★ ★

UK

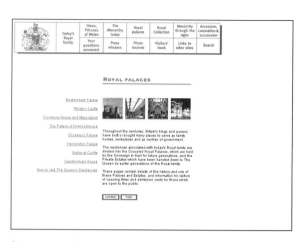

This is the location for the homepages of all the Royal residences in the UK that are open to the public. The histories and locations of Windsor Castle, Buckingham Palace, Holyrood House, Sandringham, Balmoral Castle and Frogmore House are all described on this site. The sheer size of these palaces means that the coverage is not quite as detailed as it might be. Still, getting details of this variety of palaces is some achievement. Buckingham Palace, The Queen's Gallery and the Royal Mews (Stables) receive more treatment than the other palaces, though all are well served by images of the rooms and histories of the palaces. Perhaps more importantly than the histories is the option to email for tickets; it's absolutely vital, given the queues at Buckingham Palace.

The descriptions of the individual palaces are backed up by a wonderful section on the history of the Royal Family. Here, one can find biographies of all the Royal families, dating back to the Norman Conquest and including family trees plus histories of England. There are particularly large sections on the current Queen and of course, Diana Princess of Wales features heavily. The scale of the information of this archive on the Royal Family more than matches both their longevity and the variety of their palaces.

That staple of websites, the FAQ, appears to answer such questions as 'Is the Queen the richest woman in the world?' (the answer is a qualified 'we're not going to tell you') and 'Why does the Queen keep corgis?' It seems to be Queen Victoria's fault.

Palaces, Princes, Kings and Queens, what more could a Royalist surfer want ?

OTHER SITES OF INTEREST

Hellenic Ministry of Culture
www.culture.gr/home/welcome.html
The internet has not penetrated Greece as much as it has some other areas, but this site has details of all the museums in Greece. Museums, archaeological sites and ruins can be found either through the map, which is accessible from the homepage, or the search engines. If you pick where you want to go on holiday, you can find out what's in the area you are visiting. Anyone who has experienced the glories of Ancient Athens or Olympia will understand the importance of this site.

Blenheim Palace
www.blenheimpalace.com
The home of the Duke of Marlborough and birthplace of Winston Churchill is a World Heritage site. Excellent photos make some pages a little slow to download, but can be enlarged, making this site a visual feast for anyone interested in architectural and landscape history.

Castle Howard
www.castlehoward.co.uk
This venue is famous as the setting for the TV adaptation of Brideshead Revisited. Click on The Howard Family for visual and text tours of the building and picture collection. A separate section highlights the treasures, gardens and grounds, and presents details of visiting Castle Howard and its other activities.

Chatsworth House
www.chatsworth-house.co.uk
As well as online gift shopping and visitor information for the magnificent country seat of the Duke of Devonshire, this site provides an online virtual tour of the public rooms and gardens, with accompanying text.

Jorvik Viking Centre
www.jorvik-viking-centre.co.uk
The Jorvik Viking Centre website boasts lots of spice, information and fun, starting from the charmingly enthusiastic and robust homepage. The earthiness is part of the point and charm of the museum; you can easily download sound files portraying a Viking Market and the curators bemoan that you can't yet download smells from the internet. Still, they will send you some scratch-and-sniff cards with the relevant smells on them free of charge. More practically, there is a lot of information about getting to the site and booking timed tickets in advance. For those whose interest in the Vikings extends to growing long hair and dressing up at weekends, there are details of the living history activities at the centre and nationwide.

Fire and Police Museum, Sheffield
www.hedgepig.freeserve.co.uk/
There's not much here but this site merits inclusion as being Britain's largest entirely volunteer-run museum. The site lives up to this billing with some cheerful images of fire engines and related paraphernalia. For anyone interested in this subject, follow the numerous links to a variety of fire service museums worldwide.

Galleries of Justice, UK
www.galleriesofjustice.org.uk/
A rather gloomy subject and collection has been transformed by a recent £6 million makeover, including a revamped website. The site is attractive and well laid-out, although there isn't an awful lot to it. Considering people's often ghoulish interest in crime, it is surprising that an exciting collection isn't made better use of on the site.

Hedmark Museum, Norway
www.hedmarksmuseet.museum.no/englishindex.htm
Don't be put off by the Scandinavian text; much of this website is available in English. A unique development, the Hedmark museum contains the ruins of Norway's oldest

cathedral as well as its surrounding town and fort, which were all destroyed in the 16th century. Under the largest glass canopy in Europe, visitors can take a stroll through the medieval ruins down to a lake and swimming area. Included in the complex are Herb gardens, a folklore museum, and a museum dedicated to rural life from the 17th century. Anyone planning a visit to Scandinavia should be sure to check out this site, as we're sure some of the many activities available will tickle them into a visit.

Jane Austen Museum, UK
www.janeaustenmuseum.org.uk/
Based in the house in which she wrote Pride and Prejudice, this charming little site has only a few pages that describe the history of the house and family. There are details of how to get there, along with a shop which runs a mail order business. There is not online catalogue or store, though.

Topkapi Palace, Turkey
www.ee.bilkent.edu.tr/~history/topkapi.html
This website is let down by a rather lacklustre attitude to design and images. There aren't as many images as there might be and some of them seem to take an age to download. However, the level of information is exceptionally high and detailed, making the relative paucity of the images seem quite painless.

Waddesdon Manor, UK
www.waddesdon.org.uk/
This website is surprisingly low key for a house and collection that has won numerous national awards. In particular, little is made of a lavish collection and wonderfully manicured gardens. Given recent awards won by the shop, the lack of an online store is almost as bizarre as the absence of both images and descriptions of the house and gardens.

Weald and Downland Open Air Museum, UK
www.wealddown.co.uk/home-page-english.htm
Some rather dowdy images let this site down, but if you're interested in proletarian, historic buildings then this site has dozens of images and histories for you. For children there are horses, sheep and, curiously, insects – all of them lovingly described and photographed.

have you registered for **free updates?**

log on to

www.thegoodwebguide.co.uk

Chapter 06

other peoples, other places

Here, you can find details of all those museums that take as their subject the history of peoples. Of course, all museums (except those to do with natural history) are about people to some extent, but here we're concerned with museums that have as the focus of their collections the artefacts of specific cultures and peoples. If this sounds rather convoluted, you should read articles on the distinctions between anthropology, sociology and ethnography (some of which appear on the Field Museums website). The exotic and occasionally mundane lives of Ancient Greeks, Hopi Indians, South Sea Islanders, Slavs and many more peoples can be found on the websites in this chapter.

www.fmnh.org
The Field Museum

Overall rating: ★ ★ ★ ★ ★			
Classification:	General	**Readability:**	★ ★ ★ ★ ★
Updating:	Weekly	**Content:**	★ ★ ★ ★
Navigation:	★ ★ ★	**Speed:**	★ ★ ★

UK

This museum is very difficult to categorise, its collections ranging from Classical Rome to man-eating tigers, dinosaurs and anthropology. Oh, and, at the time of review, it was hosting the Magic of Star Wars exhibition, the online version of which can be found under the Smithsonian review in Chapter 7 (see p.92). All of this is well displayed on this quick, user-friendly site. Navigation can be a little difficult, but that's only because there are so many links on each page that you aren't always sure what is a link and what isn't. Many of the links have a rather lexigraphic feel, the tone being exemplified by a 'Center for Cultural Understanding and Change'.

Don't be too put off, though: the curators at least seem to believe in the usefulness of such expressions, and the site as a whole boasts a stimulating mix of the more popular elements – dinosaurs, for example – with the serious ethnographic collections. This academic rigour is also manifested in the events section, which has a full programme of weekly lectures. If you're not burdened by children wanting to see Yoda or dinosaurs, you should certainly take advantage of these.

The museum boasts no less than four separate shops, including separate stores for dinosaur- and insect-related material. Much of the product is illustrated and described online, although none of it can be purchased online at present. Still, you can ring up and order, so the effort hasn't been entirely wasted. One other point to note – and it's one that other museums should take into consideration – is the section within planning a visit that refers to other attractions within the area. The fiasco over the UK's Millennium Dome project indicates what happens if you have an attraction in the middle of nowhere.

SPECIAL FEATURES

Sue on the Web It seems incongruous to call a Tyrannosaurus Rex 'Sue', but this is the name given to one of the best-preserved dinosaur skeletons found in America. Produced largely for children, this area has a timeline of dinosaur activity and more specific details on the Tyrannosaurus Rex. The skull is well analysed and the FAQ section is strong, so harassed parents and children writing projects might find this area useful.

Underground Adventure Using a QuickTime player, children or adults can analyse the lives of insects and plant roots. Move the viewer around using the cursor, but notice that on scrolling over certain areas you will be offered the choice to jump to another 'station' from which to explore subterranean lifestyles. We experienced some Explorer errors using these tours, but if you are patient the experience is worthwhile.

An amazingly varied and sophisticated site, featuring an occasionally bewildering range of subjects and features.

www.hunterian.gla.ac.uk/HuntMus/

The Hunterian Museum, Scotland

Overall rating: ★ ★ ★ ★ ★			
Classification: General		**Readability:**	★ ★ ★
Updating: Monthly		**Content:**	★ ★ ★ ★
Navigation: ★ ★ ★		**Speed:**	★ ★ ★

UK

An elegant and under-elaborated homepage hosts a variety of well-designed features here. There are no shops, no corporate entertainment – just lots of information and pertinent images. The permanent displays are well described, featuring images, snatches of music and highlights from the collection. Displays on Captain Cook, Ancient Egypt and Geology can be seen, among others, giving a solid and well-illustrated idea of the range of the collections.

SPECIAL FEATURES

Temporary exhibitions/Permanent Displays Many of the current, temporary exhibitions have been developed for the web – do take a look, as there are diverting treatments on Goya, Old Masters and Money. The feel of the Goya section takes his dark moods and tones a little too far, though, and the images could be bigger. This is particularly strange given how large and colourful the Roman coins in the section on Roman Architecture are; still, money probably has more lustre than sketches. Check out the previous exhibitions (there are lots of them); if you find a title that interests, the information will be pertinent and well illustrated.

Tour the Museum (Virtual & Guided) The virtual tour works smoothly and quickly; use the navigation buttons at the bottom of the screen to walk around the galleries, clicking on anything outlined in blue to find out more about each

specific object. While not as fashionable as the QuickTime approach, this gives a better idea of the collection, the space and, importantly, the lighting and displays. The image quality is high. The guided tour is just as effective, taking viewers (via a simple forward/back navigation) through the evolution of hominids via models and computer-generated images. The dense text is easily highbrow enough for those writing essays and projects.

Online Exhibition The subject could perhaps be more engaging, but the Hunterian has made good use of the web to display items from the reserve collection. Small, Neolithic 'carved stone balls' will perhaps not be of interest to all, but as a way of displaying reserve collections the internet makes perfect sense. After all, how many people likely to visit the museum will be specifically interested in 22 stone balls?

Authoritative, well-designed and varied collections help to make this one of the best sites to come out of the many museums in Scotland.

www-win.kunstkamera.lanck.ru
Kunstkamera Museum of Anthropology and Ethnography

Overall rating: ★ ★ ★ ★			
Classification: Anthropology		**Readability:**	★ ★ ★ ★
Updating: Unclear		**Content:**	★ ★ ★ ★
Navigation: ★ ★ ★		**Speed:**	★ ★

RU

A surprising inclusion, this site looks at first sight somewhat amateur. In fact, it revels in lots of information and a wonderful range of collections. We couldn't find anywhere else on the net where pictures of Scythian jewellery rub shoulders with images of conjoined twins and embalmed feet. Both can be found here in the sections on the collection and exhibitions.

The collections were started under Peter the Great and cover all the world's major ethnic groups, with an understandable focus on those of the Asian continent. Some items from the collection are illustrated in sepia tones; click on them and they expand and appear in colour. Various areas of the collection are well described, although some areas of the collection have yet to receive any descriptions at all.

The range of special exhibitions is fascinating, featuring Siberian shamans, 19th-century anatomical rarities, phalluses from Borneo and 18th-century diplomatic gifts. The anatomical collections are a marvel; unknown to the author, Peter the Great decreed that all 'monsters' should be brought to St. Petersburg to be preserved by the royal anatomist Frederick Ryusch. In the 18th century, this collection became known as the eighth wonder of the world. Although we live in slightly more enlightened times, the images are still compelling. All of the images can be expanded so that they appear in full colour; be aware that some may find the images of babies in brine a little disturbing. On a more prosaic note, there is no online shop.

An eclectic collection makes this site of interest to anyone, particularly those with a ghoulish disposition.

www.cycladic-m.gr
The Museum of Cycladic Art

Overall rating: ★ ★ ★			
Classification: Art		**Readability:**	★ ★ ★ ★
Updating: Unclear		**Content:**	★ ★ ★
Navigation: ★ ★ ★ ★		**Speed:**	★ ★
GR			

The Museum of Cycladic Art in Athens boasts the premier collection of Cycladic art in the world. Though not as well known as the archetypal black figure vases of Ancient Greece, Cycladic art is far more powerful in its mystery and beauty. Using striking images of the figurines at the heart of the collection, this private museum has created a visually impressive website. Follow links into the permanent galleries to explore this fascinating collection, which is well described and illustrated. Hover the cursor over any images and more detailed information will appear next to the image.

The current temporary display is well covered by the site with maps, pictures and an informative text. The current subject is archaeological digs under the centre of Athens, but previous examples move away from the classical theme with an account of the influence of Cycladic Art on the works of Moore and Picasso and modern interpretations of Mycenan frescoes.

SPECIAL FEATURES
Considering that Greece enjoys (or rather puts up with) over eight million tourists a year, and given that most of them pass through Athens at some point, it is curious to note how poorly developed their museum shops are. Yet here, as in so much else, the Cyclades are very well represented. The online shop features almost the entire range of reproduction statues, plates, figurines, bronzes and jewellery that can be found in the museum itself. The reproductions are more challenging than those found in the Metropolitan New York or the British Museum, as they represent a less well-known type of collection. They are reasonably priced (most under $100), given their quality, although we would like to see a reproduction of the figure that graces the homepage made available. The museum also sells a small range of publications and posters. Prices are all in dollars, and international payment is currently only by bankers draft or American Express. Payment and shipping can be arranged directly over the internet.

Wonderful images and a unique shop make this a stimulating site, and one well worth visiting.

www.peabody.harvard.edu
Peabody Museum of Archaeology and Ethnology

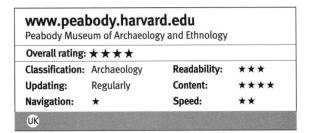

Overall rating: ★ ★ ★ ★			
Classification:	Archaeology	**Readability:**	★ ★ ★
Updating:	Regularly	**Content:**	★ ★ ★ ★
Navigation:	★	**Speed:**	★ ★

UK

An elegantly simple homepage greets the visitor to this offshoot of Harvard University. We found the links smooth, although the navigation is rather complex. This is largely due to the variety and amount of material that there is on the site. Follow links to the individual departments to explore information on peoples as diverse as Enuit Eskimos and Peruvian Indians. The lives of these people are explored using archives, photographic resources and online exhibitions. The coverage varies between different people and areas but is generally of a high quality and detailed.

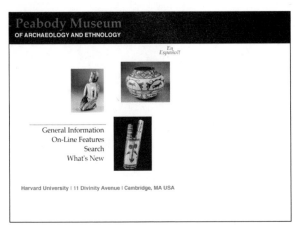

There is a massive account of the Copán culture from South America, including a QuickTime display explaining its history, current excavations, notable collections and currently visitable sites. Not every department has the same level of detail, but the account of the Copán gives a sense of the kind of serious treatment of ethnographic subjects you can find on the site.

SPECIAL FEATURES

Online Features The archives and exhibitions here should constitute a compulsory resource for anyone seriously studying the development of modern anthropology. As well as accounts of the travels and acquisitions of the founders of American Ethnology in 'The Ethnography of Lewis and Clark', their extensive archive is fully described and catalogued, with many objects illustrated. This historical attitude is set off by a thoroughly modern account of running and runners. Taking as its staring point Hopi Indians' ceremonial running, it explores 19th-century runners and the development of the major competitions as well as boasting links to running clubs for the more athletically motivated surfer to join. All of this is well-illustrated and conceived, making this a compelling, contemporary treatment of anthropology.

Gargantuan and highly rigorous in its standards.

www.rom.on.ca
Royal Ontario Museum

Overall rating: ★ ★ ★ ★			
Classification:	General	Readability:	★ ★ ★ ★
Updating:	Regularly	Content:	★ ★ ★ ★
Navigation:	★ ★ ★	Speed:	★ ★

CAN

An intriguing mix of art, natural history and archaeology characterises this site. Visitors can meet a Maiasaur (a type of dinosaur), view the largest collection of Korean art in the Americas and explore Geo in the Earth Sciences Gallery. In the Dynamic Earth exhibition you can experience the bizarre sensation of listening to talking rocks, as ammonite offers a particularly interesting account of its life (this runs easily enough with QuickTime). As befits a museum of national standing the links work efficiently. As with many of the sites reviewed here, though, the size of the site and the sheer number of links can be overwhelming.

Probably the best way to navigate around the site is to use the quick and efficient search facility, which directs browsers to a variety of different galleries and tours. For example, the Egyptian and Greek galleries contain a series of film clips, shots of the collection and objects to explain the collections and their significance. The film clips are particularly impressive, with footage of ancient ruins punctuated by clips of enthusiastic curators explaining a particular theme or object. A tip for those using slower modems: if you download the less memory intensive version, the picture or sound quality is not impaired and the download is quicker. The enthusiasm of the curators gives these galleries a power and interest unmatched by many others we've seen. Indeed, it's probably much better than actually visiting the museum and showing yourself around.

Of more strictly academic significance, the museum describes its involvement in the Nakavona Cave excavation, presenting a series of reports from an excavation funded by the Royal Ontario Museum on the coast of Croatia. The tone is scholarly and the text is worth reading for anyone interested in the gritty and often rain-soaked practicalities of archaeology.

The shop's extensive range of reproductions (from ancient Egyptian Scarabs to 16th-century Vases), books and jewellery are well described on the site, but orders can only be emailed or telephoned.

SPECIAL FEATURES

Ancient Egypt Follow the link on the homepage to the Ancient Egyptian discovery case (the weather-beaten looking suitcase). The Egyptian department seems to have made a huge effort to present as much material as possible in as stimulating a way as possible. Although it has been designed with children and teachers in mind, as is the way with these things, it is full of information and images for anyone interested in Ancient Egypt. You can send postcards from the site, choosing from a wide range of images from their 'post rack'. The images are of items from the collection, and they are all sharp and arresting.

In keeping with the museum's status as one of the foremost in Canada, the website is lively and fascinating.

www.ashmol.ox.ac.uk
Ashmolean Museum

Overall rating: ★ ★ ★ ★			
Classification: Archaeology		**Readability:**	★ ★ ★
Updating: Regularly		**Content:**	★ ★ ★
Navigation: ★ ★ ★		**Speed:**	★ ★ ★ ★ ★

UK

A curate's egg of a website, this merits inclusion for the interest of some of its features. The descriptions of the collections departments are derisory given the quality of the collection. The classical holdings are too good to be described in two sentences. This is, of course, surely due to lack of time and funding rather than lack of ambition. The brass rubbings are well documented with an online catalogue, which includes images. The object of the month actually is changed every month, and the maker or artist is described alongside a history and analysis of the piece. There are also details of related objects in the collection. The choices we've seen reflect the broad range of the collection from antiquity to the 19th century.

SPECIAL FEATURES

POTWEB This is a pilot website, which illustrates much of the museum's medieval and later pottery collection. It is introduced by a series of discussions explaining the significance of pots and pottery for archaeologists and historians. The level of information is high and there are more images than in the rest of the site – but, to be honest, the overall impact is low.

Brass Rubbings Catalogue Like POTWEB, we feel that this endeavour is probably a bit too specialist to make much of an impact. But for those interested in brass rubbings, we can see it becoming a positive Mecca. Here is a catalogue of the 5,000 or so brass rubbings kept by the museum (in storage). This list is broken down into parish, which should be useful to people who research this sort of thing. There is also a gallery showing many rubbings from the collection.

FAQs These are far more interesting than usual. There is detailed information on the history of the Ashmolean, conservation techniques, and two of the most important items in the collection: the Blendell Prism and the Metrological Relief are excellently described and analysed.

Some very good, some not so good; be sure to look and decide for yourself.

www.fitzmuseum.cam.ac.uk

The Fitzwilliam Museum, Cambridge

Overall rating: ★ ★ ★ ★			
Classification:	Academic	Readability:	★ ★ ★ ★
Updating:	Monthly	Content:	★ ★ ★ ★
Navigation:	★ ★ ★ ★	Speed:	★ ★ ★ ★

UK

Despite its quizzical looking owl (do owls ever look anything else?), the homepage for Cambridge University's museum looks rather bland. However, explore a bit and you will find lots of information along with a rather nice exhibition of the works of Turner. The collections and special exhibitions are described in adequate detail with some images, alongside extensive details of the lecture and seminar program. The gallery map is good, although again, more information on the collections would be useful. There is a full calendar of gallery talks as well as many temporary exhibitions, which can be found by following the link from the homepage. If this sort of thing interests you, check the education page.

SPECIAL FEATURES

Virtual Turner Although Ruskin chose to give the majority of his extensive collection of Turners to his alma mater Oxford, he left an important collection of 25 Turner landscapes to Cambridge. This exhibition works well as an introduction to Ruskin and Turner, and each landscape is described and analysed. The quality of the collection fully deserves this caring approach.

The Turner landscapes alone manage to give this site a heavyweight presence.

www.museumoflondon.org.uk

Museum of London

Overall rating: ★ ★ ★ ★			
Classification:	Archaeology	Readability:	★ ★ ★ ★
Updating:	Biweekly	Content:	★ ★ ★ ★
Navigation:	★ ★ ★	Speed:	★ ★ ★ ★

UK

Available in English, Dutch, Spanish and Italian, the main strengths of this site are its coverage of the archaeological work and collections of the museum and its associated archaeological unit. Anyone interested in the day-to-day, unglamorous work of archaeologists will spend hours here.

All the collection areas are described with some arresting images; certainly the Mickey Mouse gas mask from the Second World War would interest any child. Follow the links to the Macabre London tour for some ghoulish pictures of pagan sacrifices, or at least some skeletal remains that may or may not be of unwilling participants in some ritual. This interest in the macabre is to be maintained with future exhibitions planned on gladiators, burial practices and 19th-century photographs of cemeteries. You can see why we mention the Mickey Mouse gas mask.

Details of the many past exhibitions and those currently on show can be found under the exhibitions link, though it is a pity that none of the forthcoming exhibitions are on the site in much detail. There is no online shop but you can email a catalogue request.

SPECIAL FEATURES

High Street Londinium Rather interestingly, the Banca di Roma, doubtless wishing to highlight past glories, sponsors this event. It would be intriguing to see if the National Bank of Greece would sponsor an exhibition on the Elgin Marbles in the same spirit. It would be nice to be able to take some kind of virtual tour around the streets of a reconstructed Londinium (as one can in the exhibition itself) but the online version is still full of lots of detail and information about the Romans in the capital. This would be a godsend to harassed parents trying to come up with information for projects, as the online sections contain broader views of the Romans in Britain and archaeology in general.

Remembering the Blitz A well-designed feature, this area covers the history of the Blitz and, more interestingly, modern responses and memories. Indeed, those who lived through it are encouraged to email their memories to the exhibition designers, which is a nice use of the web to interact with and shape an exhibition.

Far more varied in its collections and approach than its name and erstwhile subject might suggest.

www.prm.ox.ac.uk
Pitt Rivers Museum

Overall rating: ★ ★ ★

Classification:	Anthropology	Readability:	★★★★
Updating:	Monthly	Content:	★★★
Navigation:	★★★	Speed:	★★★

UK

At first view, this is a rather worthy site for what is a wonderfully esoteric collection. The download is quick, largely due to a disappointing lack of images on the title and basic information pages. With objects ranging from shrunken heads to totem poles, the collection should have received a greater emphasis on the initial or 'grabbing' pages. The site is divided into regulation sections on opening times, admissions (free) and the like. The borders are framed by patterns from various ethnic backgrounds, which contrast with the rather plain white spaces of the pages. The lack of bright colours and moving images betokens the individualistic approach of this site; no corporate marketing/website designers have been at work here. There is no online shop (there is information on research publications) nor ticket booking facility; although since tickets are free and the shop is minute, this is no great loss. What the site does have in its favour is that it assumes a level of interest and intelligence which many cultural sites do not, making it a rewarding visit even if you've never had any great interest in anthropology.

SPECIAL FEATURES

Introduction to the Collection The main strength of the site lies in this area. Requiring more of the viewer than the content on most museum sites, it contains overviews of the Cook Collection, the Japanese Collection, and the museum's Collection of Native American Photographs. A section on the museum's Collection of Musical Instruments is under construction (the bane of museum websites). These pages detailed and well illustrated, although the pictures are small and slow to appear. Both the pictures and the text are sharp and unusual enough to titillate the viewer into wanting to explore the subject and the site further. One only hopes that they can do the same for other areas of the collection.

History of the Museum The life story and character of Pitt Rivers provides a fascinating background to the style and content of the museum. This section would improve with more images, although these sections use the internet's ability to display information in a pick-and-mix way very well. Quotations are used to good effect, presenting Rivers as one of the first people to think deeply about museum display. Overall, it's a useful corrective to the mission speak that can be found on many other museum sites.

A superb collection is well-displayed and explained on this charmer of a site.

www.ncl.ac.uk/shefton-museum
Shefton Museum

Overall rating: ★ ★ ★			
Classification:	Archaeology	**Readability:**	★ ★ ★
Updating:	Regularly	**Content:**	★ ★ ★ ★
Navigation:	★ ★	**Speed:**	★ ★ ★

UK

Hosted by Newcastle University and maintained by its Classics staff, this site has plenty of information that is seriously explained and well-displayed. Much of the site is currently under construction (notably, the section on life in the Ancient Greek World), but if what has been completed so far is a guide, the rest of the site will be fine indeed.

The series of essays on military themes in Greek Archaeology – such as Greek armour – are well illustrated, with artefacts from the collection sitting alongside a useful glossary of classical terms. Teachers can find class notes and handouts, while the details of various conferences also appear on the site. These vary from the detailed not to say obscure, like 'Siculo-geometric and the Sikels: Ceramics and identity in eastern Sicily' to those which will be of interest to the more general reader. The site might benefit from some money being spent on a professional designer, as the current look is a trifle amateur, but the combination of enthusiasm with scholarly rigour works well. Like a similar project at the Ashmolean, the Shefton Museum is well served by a passion for the classics, which transmits well throughout the site. Children and hardened academics could both find material of use here.

SPECIAL FEATURES

Ostia Dedicated to the Ancient Roman port of Ostia, this site, hosted by the Shefton museum, contains maps, discussion documents and lots of sumptuous photographs of this important classical site. You have to register to use many of the site's facilities, but it is well worth the effort as the site represents a forum for numerous scholars in the field. For those just wanting an introduction to Ostia, prior to a trip to Rome, to those seriously interested in Classical Archaeology, this forum has much to offer.

Serious yet enthusiastic, and ideal for anyone interested in the Classics.

OTHER SITES OF INTEREST

Archaeological Museum of Bologna, Italy
www.comune.bologna.it/bologna/Musei/Archeologico/welcom_e.htm
Though some of the translation on this website may need polishing, the museum merits attention for its wonderful Etruscan and Roman collections. Not all of the content has been translated into English, but the information illuminates the history of Classical-period northern Italy very well indeed, using many images from the collections and excavations. Anyone planning a visit to Bologna should pay attention to the thematic tours described in the museum; these allow visitors to pursue individual themes through the objects displayed on the web. The online book shop contains many Italian titles describing the Egyptian and Classical collections, including a couple in English, which can be ordered online – provided you understand Italian.

Bethnal Green Museum of Childhood, UK
www.vam.ac.uk/Infodome/
It's a shame that this museum doesn't have its own website. Instead, it is buried in the Victoria & Albert's site. It has no images and the information is minimal, which is a pity given that the museum itself is rather pleasant.

Etruscan Virtual Museum
www.agmen.com/etruscans/index.htm
This rather idiosyncratic site doesn't seem to be linked to any museum or academic institution, but it does have some fascinating details of that most enigmatic of ancient peoples – the Etruscans – as well as some fabulous images. Follow the cartoon Etruscan, Larth, around the principal Etruscan sites and you can read general accounts of Etruscan origins, lives and beliefs. Anyone planning to visit Italy – particularly those with small children – should definitely have a look at this, if only to put the magnificent Etruscan remains into some sort of context. Anyone whose interest runs to buying reproduction Etruscan knick-knacks could spend quite a lot

of time and money in the online store. If you've got that itch to decorate your home with frescoes and statues in an Etruscan rather than Tuscan style, you can shop safely with your credit card here.

Norske Folkemuseum, Norway
www.norskfolke.museum.no/
Don't be put off by all the Norwegian on the left-hand side of the page, just click on the English icon at the top of the page and follow the links at the bottom of the page. This opens up all the links in Norwegian on the left-hand side of the page. Through them you can explore this museum of Norwegian buildings and folk culture, in which a 1920s gas station jostles with Sami shamans for the visitor's attention.

The Petrie Museum, London
www.petrie.ucl.ac.uk
This museum is as hard to find on the web as it is physically. Despite a moderately publicised commissioning of a modern artist to design the site, not enough thought has been given to making it easy to track down. Unfortunately, the artist doesn't seem to have started his work. Still, the site is competent enough, with an overview of the collections and their history, some particular objects being described and illustrated. We will be going back soon to see if they've changed much.

Whitby Museum
www.durain.demon.co.uk
Run by the Whitby Literary and Philosophical Society, this charming site is devoted to the history and people of this north-east town. We've suffered lots of poor local and regional museums, but this site shows how a few dedicated people can achieve impressive results.

Chapter 07

planes, trains and automobiles

Unlike the higher brow museums of design, art and history, the sites in this chapter tend to inspire a peculiar enthusiasm. While great art often seems to be above reproach, museums devoted to more practical areas of human endeavour tend to speak more directly to their constituencies. Train museums don't display any shame about the existence of trainspotters, while military museums engage the small boy who thrills at guns, however politically incorrect some might find it. Specifications and technical details expressed as reams of abbreviations and figures can be found all over these sites, like the careless droppings from some great machine god. In short, these are the museums you will either love or hate.

www.nasm.si.edu
The Smithsonian National Air and Space Museum

Overall rating: ★ ★ ★ ★ ★			
Classification:	Air/Space	**Readability:**	★ ★ ★ ★ ★
Updating:	Regularly	**Content:**	★ ★ ★ ★ ★
Navigation:	★ ★ ★	**Speed:**	★ ★ ★

US

The Smithsonian Institute covers a massive variety of museums, research centres and galleries – not forgetting a zoo – some of which can be found elsewhere in this book. The National Air and Space Museum is one of the most famous, and it has one of the most extensive sites. The visitor information is comprehensive and includes the schedule of renovation and repair, which should be compulsory on all major museum sites. Potential visitors should also note the gallery maps, which offer detailed plans guiding visitors to their favourite items in the collection. If you click on the relevant themes, these gallery plans also provide a conceptual overview of the gallery and its objects.

The overviews are well written and informative, and would be useful for children writing projects on areas relating to aviation or space. They're not all of the same length or detail (compare the patchy coverage of the Second World War to the much fuller and more stimulating treatment of astronomy) but offer valuable coverage before or after any visit to the museum.

Details of the Albert Einstein Planetarium and the IMAX cinema within the NASM are not given in such detail, but viewing times and schedules of daily events can be found on the site. Given American familiarity with internet shopping, it is surprising to find that the online shop for the museum has such a small product range. It seems more interested in plugging the large model of the Star Trek space ship in its display cabinets than in the full range of books on aviation history that the shop carries. More aviation-related products appear in the main Smithsonian Online Shop but a desultory three items doesn't do the range and size of the NASM shop justice. Still, you can order goods online and the server is secure, although international postage is not guaranteed.

The site also contains details of the Udvar-Hazy centre, a new outdoor development which would house many of the biggest aircraft from the Museum's collection. Extensive details are given of the planning process and proposed features. However, currently it would only be of interest to those planning rival aircraft museums.

SPECIAL FEATURES

Online Gallery – Star Wars This exhibition was held at the Smithsonian to mark the release of a new film in

the series in 1999. The show is now on tour but the Smithsonian has released this online version, which will apparently run indefinitely. Using QuickTime and voiceovers from some of the original artists, this exhibition takes you through the mythology and philosophy behind the hugely successful films. Storyboards, costumes, concept art, clips and stills all develop the concepts behind the film and will be of great interest to anyone sold on the phenomenon of Star Wars.

Online Exhibition, Apollo to the Moon This is really just an expanded version of the full gallery guides noted above, but it is no less effective for that. It tells the story of the race to the moon, starting with Kennedy's pronouncement in 1961. It also lays out the background to Kennedy's decision and the effects of lunar exploration, and includes a massive list of artefacts in the museum's collection that were connected with the project. Most importantly, though, it contains links to some of the other gallery tours within the museum, so that following a Cold War link brings one to the gallery called Space Race.

As with many of the US sites, there are lots of features and interactive options here, many aimed specifically at children.

www.iwm.org.uk/lambeth/index.htm
Imperial War Museum

Overall rating: ★ ★ ★ ★			
Classification:	Military	**Readability:**	★ ★ ★ ★
Updating:	Regularly	**Content:**	★ ★ ★ ★
Navigation:	★ ★ ★	**Speed:**	★ ★ ★

UK

Slightly confusingly, the Imperial War Museum homepage also covers the pages for the Cabinet War Rooms and the Fleet Air arm museum. The remit of the Imperial War Museum is quite specific in covering Military Affairs after 1914; those looking for other periods should look at the National Army Museum. Within this period, the museum's site is packed with information about the collections and displays. The visitor information is full and furnished with two detailed maps, and if the permanent collections could be described in more detail, the facilities for scholars are at least well covered. The permanent collections receive illustrated overviews that really only scratch the surface of the subject; they would benefit from the more enthusiastic approach of the online exhibitions (see below).

The shop has a limited range of goods illustrated online (almost entirely Churchill Memorabilia), and ordering is via telephone or printed form. Some of the museum's handbooks and gallery guides appear throughout the site and are also available in the same way. Details are given of the extensive printed materials produced by the Government and a full catalogue is downloadable in Adobe Acrobat format. This looks too specialist for the general reader, but for a serious researcher both this and the list of combat maps would be an invaluable resource.

Online Exhibitions The variety of these online exhibitions gives a good impression of the breadth of this museum. It's not just tanks and guns for bearded military enthusiasts, a wide range of social history is covered in exhibitions on the Holocaust and the experience of Mass Industry during the Second World War. These exhibitions are largely descriptions of the physical exhibitions, with added information describing specific concepts or results. The most interesting use of the medium are the taped reminiscences from Korean war veterans. The clips are short and play easily on any of the higher RealPlayer downloads. Those interviewed have suffered the full range of wartime experiences and are movingly matter of fact about warfare and imprisonment during the conflict. This approach should be made more widespread as it is not too memory intensive and brings the past to life.

Given the two recent films (U-571 and Enigma), it would be surprising if the Enigma coding machine did not make an appearance. It has its own online exhibition here, and the history of military codes is traced with a good selection of images from the First World War onwards. A selection of games and puzzles for children are also included.

'Imperial' and 'war' must be two of the most derided words in the modern political lexicon, and the museum is slightly too cowed by them. Still, although the IWM should be more forthright in describing and explaining their collections, the site does have much to offer.

www.nmm.ac.uk
National Maritime Museum

Overall rating: ★ ★ ★ ★

Classification:	Sea Travel	Readability:	★ ★ ★
Updating:	Regularly	Content:	★ ★ ★ ★
Navigation:	★ ★ ★	Speed:	★ ★ ★

UK

As the homepage proudly declares, this is really three museums in one – and the website certainly boasts enough content for three museums. As well as the maritime elements, the Royal Observatory and the Queen's house are well represented. The history of the Queen's house and its inhabitants are described, along with images of the royalty closely associated with it. Timelines and biographies further illustrate the history of the royal family and, as with the royal palaces site discussed in Chapter 5, the family themselves are covered more thoroughly than the property.

There are extensive picture resources, plus a large education and children's area to go with the more mundane maps, visiting instructions and the like. Navigation can appear confusing, due largely to the plethora of choices available, but drop-down menus, hotlinks and navigation arrows actually all move the viewer smoothly through the pages. It can be slightly difficult to find exactly what you are looking for because the majority of the links take you to the more academic areas of the site, notably the massive library and picture collections.

The children's area could be fuller (it has instructions for making telescopes and a mask) but it is supplemented by quizzes, which are good fun and can be taxing – the author's ships sank twice! Included in the adults' and children's section are a series of fact files, covering such disparate subjects as Nelson and vikings as well as providing useful commentary on the main displays. These would be useful for young students (say, under-16s) who are writing projects.

SPECIAL FEATURES

PORT Online Search Facility Within the Centre for Maritime Research there are a large number of links to various educational resources, by far the most significant of which is PORT. It is an engine that searches maritime internet resources, so the potential range of information is massive. The search is quick and the results are pertinent, so the museum is to be commended for providing online access to this resource. This facility is complemented by exhaustive research notes and bibliographies, which are broken down into themes and chronologies. The academic rigour is maintained by the regular production of the electronic Journal of Naval History.

We haven't found a better site for researching naval matters, even among the American ones. Still, although it caters for children, it could perhaps do more to keep them occupied.

www.beaulieu.co.uk
National Motor Museum

Overall rating: ★ ★ ★ ★			
Classification:	Cars	**Readability:**	★ ★ ★ ★
Updating:	Regularly	**Content:**	★ ★ ★
Navigation:	★ ★ ★ ★	**Speed:**	★ ★ ★

UK

A quick-loading opening page takes you to a solid-enough website for this Hampshire-based motoring museum. The museum dates back to 1952, when it was called the Montagu Motor Museum. These days, it collects, preserves and presents vehicles relating to the history of motoring in Great Britain from 1895 – and further back, seemingly, given that one ride at the museum takes you as far back as the invention of the wheel – to the present day. Beaulieu bulges with more than 250 vehicles and tens of thousands of related objects – it's a lot of wheel power, in short.

But while the museum claims to be the best day out in England, the website falls just short of the full five stars, being an introduction to the museum rather than a fully-fledged online experience in itself. Still, it can't be faulted for ease of use and clarity, with three options to choose from on its opening page (the National Motor Museum and its two sibling attractions, the Beaulieu Abbey or Palace House) and a menu down the left-hand side of the screen once you're in. It never quite motors, but it's a smooth cruise.

SPECIAL FEATURES

The Motor Collection Browse what's on show at the museum by car. Nine out of ten of the vehicles we randomly checked were still 'awaiting photograph', which makes the site pretty self-explanatory: get yourself down to Hampshire if you're after the full caboodle.

Automobilia is an introduction to some of the additional accessories and automobile-aids at the museum. What the site does offer is some automobilia desktop wallpaper, sure to bring keen car lovers out in a hot flush every time they turn on their computer.

Jack Tucker's Garage Trek back in time and check out this 1930s garage, complete with rusty drainpipe.

Interactive Gallery We got a bit excited here, thinking there would be some QuickTime or RealPlayer audio-visual action to be had. Alas, it's merely blurb for what you'll find at the museum, where, apparently, you can try out different forms of suspension by bouncing up and down on them.

Rides and Drives Enticing blurb for the crazy things you can do in Hampshire, like take a trip in a space-age pod from the first Stone Age wheels to a vision of what cars in the future might look like.

Education Find out about educational possibilities via their online educational booking form.

Palace House Link on the opening page to the 14th-century Great Gatehouse of Beaulieu Abbey. Take a not-entirely state-of-the-art virtual tour, salivate over the Victorian menus (roast this, roast that) and meet the Montagu family's famous ancestors.

Beaulieu Abbey This place was founded in 1204 by Cistercian monks on land given to them by King John. Follow the Exploring the Abbey link to find out what went on where around the grounds; click on the section you're interested in with your mouse. Alternatively, click on Ghosts! to find out which ethereal individuals are still loitering in the cloisters. Apparently, visitors have been known to ask why The Grey Lady won't speak to them.... it's because she's dead.

Not exactly cutting-edge, but a slick, efficient introduction to Beaulieu's unrivalled exploration of motoring history.

www.nmsi.ac.uk/nrm
National Railway Museum

Overall rating: ★ ★ ★ ★			
Classification:	Trains	Readability:	★ ★ ★ ★ ★
Updating:	Regular	Content:	★ ★ ★ ★
Navigation:	★ ★ ★	Speed:	★ ★ ★ ★

UK

Even if you're not a train enthusiast, it would be difficult not to be charmed by this site. Like the National Maritime Museum the NRM acts as a portal for train-related resources worldwide, boasting a very large collection of train timetables, plans, documents, pictures, posters and portraits which includes many from America and Europe. Coupled with the extensive range of links, these make this a first stop for any railway enthusiast using the web.

The language is friendly and engaging, and on many pages little loops of sepia film footage play; people play cards frenetically on a train, while on another page steam locomotive wheels turn perpetually. These touches exemplify the numerous attractions and displays of the site itself, as well as offering a portal to numerous other train sites worldwide. The large collection of trains is complemented by recent reconstructions of sidings, engineering works, a station and a turntable, while the huge array of associated memorabilia and models are kept in the Warehouse (part of the major new redisplay). All of this is lovingly described and illustrated in the Works section. Plus, for the true enthusiast, there are all-embracing technical details of the hundreds of trains within the collection.

One slight quibble: it seems odd, given how much effort has been made within the museum to appeal to children (free train rides, a playground, quizzes, a lot of interactivity in the new galleries), that no effort seems to have been made on the site itself. Teacher packs corresponding to various key stages are available, but this doesn't seem quite enough.

SPECIAL FEATURES

Online Tour The museum has been honest in calling these QuickTime feature panoramas rather than tours. A tour implies a progression or movement, whereas these facilities only allow the viewer to remain on one spot. Here, the program gives a good feel for the different galleries.

Exhiblets It is not clear whether this is a typo (it appears all over the site) or a hitherto unknown expression denoting a diminutive exhibition. The latter would seem to be the case but it is slightly misleading – the exhibitions of posters and photographs from the 1920s and 1930s are replete with images and stimulating detail.

An ideal site for any rail enthusiast, this also boasts enough to entertain others, particularly those planning a visit.

www.rafmuseum.co.uk
Royal Air Force Museum

Overall rating: ★ ★ ★ ★			
Classification:	Military	Readability:	★ ★ ★
Updating:	Regularly	Content:	★ ★ ★ ★
Navigation:	★ ★ ★	Speed:	★ ★ ★

UK

The throb of a spitfire engine taking off greets the visitor to this homepage. Once inside, any plane enthusiast would find much to inform and entertain. Follow the red links on the left-hand side of the page to find the collections, archives and details on the museum's location; all are described in comprehensive detail. This level of detail is backed up by a gallery containing more than 200 images of the planes from the collection and QuickTime tours. The image quality is high though slightly dark, as if the pictures were taken on a cloudy day; still, the images do provide comprehensive coverage of the history of flight.

For serious researchers there are full accounts of the picture, uniform, document and medal archives, with contact details and numerous links to other resources. In particular, anyone trying to research the history of a family member or friend who served within the RAF would be very well served by the links to associations, societies and similar organisations. Children are certainly well catered for within the museum itself, with a variety of games and activities. Unfortunately, these are described but not accessible online. There is a simple, downloadable game involving flying red cross parcels but it would not hold a child's attention for long.

SPECIAL FEATURES

Virtual Tours These require the ubiquitous QuickTime Player. However, once they are installed the tours run

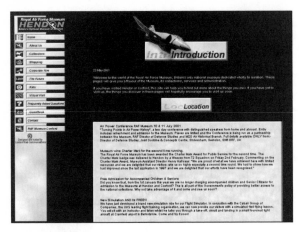

quickly and easily, and are used more effectively than at many other sites. You can stand next to a Second World War bomber, and stand inside a Sunderland flying boat; the latter option is particularly effective. There are currently three tours and plans for at least three more.

Great fun, but the museum itself has even more to do and see, especially for children.

www.invalides.org
Les Invalides

Overall rating: ★ ★ ★			
Classification:	Military	**Readability:**	★ ★
Updating:	Unclear	**Content:**	★ ★
Navigation:	★ ★ ★	**Speed:**	★ ★ ★ ★

(FR)

The National Army Museum Paris is most famous for housing Napoleon Bonaparte's burial place, and only the sections of the French website concerned with the First World War have been translated into English. This is a pity because the French language site is full and informative. The sections on the First World War consist of text with links to images from the new gallery. The text is articulate and the analysis sophisticated, but the whole is somewhat undermined by some terrible translation. The First World War did not have 'tree causes', and 'motionless warfare' seems to be a rather dodgy concept. Invalides is currently undergoing a renovation and it is to be hoped that the site will be similarly redeveloped soon.

Its arresting account of the First World War aside, this site doesn't make much of an important collection or its Napoleonic connections.

www.ltmuseum.co.uk
The London Transport Museum

Overall rating: ★ ★ ★			
Classification:	Transport	Readability:	★ ★ ★
Updating:	Monthly	Content:	★ ★ ★
Navigation:	★ ★ ★	Speed:	★ ★

UK

A tremendously bustling and full homepage greets browsers here. Options flood the screen and you have to scroll down for a good while to reach the bottom. The displays and the collection details are described in somewhat less than full detail, although this is in keeping with the light tone of the site as a whole. There are, however, details of the research and study collections available, and the collection area contains more images than the rest of the site.

The homepage also contains a link to a webcam that is set up just outside the London Transport Museum in Covent Garden. It is only updated every 45 seconds, so you have to wait for any significant action; but it is all part of the upbeat feel to the site. The full schedule of family and adult events is just as vibrant, and anyone planning a visit should definitely check it to see if they can coincide with one of the special activities. There are Kidzones throughout the London Transport Museum and the tone is maintained on the website. The history of transport in the capital is explored in child-friendly tones, with lots of pictures and cartoons. Children should be particularly amused by the FAQs, which are full of statistics about the number of rivets in the underground system and the like.

There is an online shop, but it is quite difficult to find; follow links to the shop and then click on the picture of the bus. The shop stocks numerous posters and assorted London Transport memorabilia. Prices are quoted in pounds sterling but note that the museum admits that if you use the online form your credit card details will not be encrypted.

The online exhibition, Sun a-shine, Rain a-fall, describes the experiences of West Indians who came to work for London Transport in the 1950s and 1960s. It works very well, and the text is full of pertinent pictures and personal reminiscences. Navigation is via a 'Next' button at the bottom of the screen.

A lively and very child-friendly site.

www.argylls.co.uk

Museum of the Argyll and Sutherland Highlanders at Stirling Castle

Overall rating: ★★★

Classification:	Military	**Readability:**	★★★★★
Updating:	Annual	**Content:**	★★★
Navigation:	★★★★	**Speed:**	★★★★

UK

As a regiment with a proud and historic tradition, it is fitting that the Argyll and Sutherland Highlanders (not their original appellation; the regimental re-formings and combinings are fully explained on the site) should have easily the best of the United Kingdom's regimental sites. For a full list of regimental and other military museums, see the 24-hour museum site review in chapter 8 (see p.113).

Navigation is via a list of dates and themes on the left-hand side of the screen. Though the chronological divisions can seem a little strange, these links offer a compelling history of the regiment. The narrative is tremendous, embellished with campaign maps and a suitably partisan approach to military history. Victories are trumpeted and defeats underplayed. All the major campaigns of the last two centuries appear, as the Highlanders were at the forefront of the Napoleonic and imperial wars of the 19th century. The abiding concern of this regimental history seems to be the Highlanders' desire to keep their kilts, largely in the face of Anglo-Saxon administrative indifference. Highland resolve is played up in the account of the 'thin red line' at Balaclava; typically, this great success is less well known than the disaster that followed it, the Charge of the Light Brigade.

For those stirred by stories of derring-do, there is a small mail-order catalogue (orders by phone only) plus a list of events at the castle and throughout the UK.

A wonderfully vivid site covering the history of one of the most distinctive regiments in the British – or any – army.

www.national-army-museum.ac.uk

National Army Museum

Overall rating: ★ ★ ★			
Classification:	Military	**Readability:**	★ ★ ★
Updating:	Regularly	**Content:**	★ ★
Navigation:	★ ★ ★	**Speed:**	★ ★ ★

UK

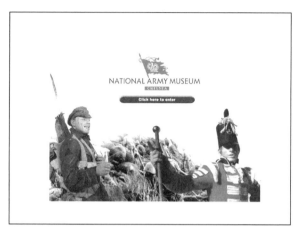

The layout and navigation of this site is pleasingly simple, with the uncluttered approach of the homepage setting the tone. This simplicity comes at a price, though, and it seems that there is not as much to the website as there could be. The galleries, collections and special exhibits are adequately described, but there are no gallery maps, or even enough detail and images, to support the value of the collection. The Education section hints at the resources of the museum, which really should be used more expansively on the site. Images of staff dressed as First World War soldiers or nurses only draws attention to the scarcity of these sorts of images in the gallery tour itself.

The calendar of gallery talks (weekly) is useful for those planning a visit, as are the descriptions of the special exhibits. Still, if you compare it with the Imperial War Museum (admittedly a larger organisation), greater resources ought to be available. For those pursuing serious research, the accounts of the library facilities and the links section would prove very useful if they had hotlinks to other military museums and archives. The online book shop is currently unavailable; we can only hope that they are in the process of creating one, so watch this space. Given the selection available in the shop at the site, an online shop would surely become an important resource for those interested in military history.

As the national museum of the subject, this website deserves respect; still, check out the Highland and Sutherlanders website in this chapter for a soldier's site with more gusto.

www.tankmuseum.co.uk/home.html
The National Tank Museum, Bovington

Overall rating: ★ ★ ★			
Classification:	Military	**Readability:**	★ ★ ★ ★
Updating:	Monthly	**Content:**	★ ★ ★
Navigation:	★ ★	**Speed:**	★ ★ ★

UK

This site merits a place here for two entirely contrary reasons. If you are interested in tanks then it contains a lot of attractively laid-out information; if you're not interested in tanks, it allows you a glimpse into a rather obsessive world. The site contains Reviews, Details of the Library and Photo Archive, Special Events, and a small online shop, all in a pleasingly simple style. There are lots of illustrations, though these are usually small and not terribly sharp, while the text is full of weights and measurements that presumably mean a lot to certain people. The FAQs section answers all sorts of questions about tanks, which you won't have realised you were interested in until you see the answers. The information does make an impact and you find yourself warming to an initially unprepossessing subject.

A minority interest, perhaps, but still one that is well catered for here.

www.zeppelin-museum.de
Zeppelin Museum

Overall rating: ★ ★ ★			
Classification:	Air Travel	**Readability:**	★ ★ ★ ★ ★
Updating:	Regularly	**Content:**	★ ★ ★
Navigation:	★ ★ ★ ★	**Speed:**	★ ★ ★

GE

This is an attractive site for a museum with an intriguing and unique collection. The grey backgrounds play host to a variety of text and images describing the history of the Air Balloon flight, the development of German commercial Zeppelins and the personalities involved. Navigation is via hotlinks and a scrollable list of options on the left-hand side of each page. All the links work quickly and the download is fast. Follow the temporary exhibitions link on the homepage to find a series of expositions on subjects that are rather tenuously linked to the theme of zeppelins (the museum plays host to various artists' work on a temporary basis). Look under School projects, via the Service option, and you will get to see a charming account of Graf von Zeppelin's life and career, with pictures of him and his family, as well as an account of the production of the exhibition.

SPECIAL FEATURES

Online Shop If you ignore the odd phraseology the shop has an unusual range of attractively presented products. There is plenty of the usual museum fare – key rings, T-shirts, caps and the like – as well as a wide range of books, journals and papers about Zeppelins. Some of the more obscure book choices are only available in German but if you're that into Zeppelins you probably read German anyway. Prices are all quoted in euros, with the mark not appearing at all, which is very forward looking of the Germans. There is currently an Antiques section under construction but it is difficult to say whether these will be Antiques or cunningly mistranslated reproductions; we will have to wait and see. The shop runs on a secure server and accepts all the usual credit cards.

A wonderfully evocative site which covers a little-understood aspect of 20th-century life between the wars.

www.armouries.org.uk/leeds/index.html
Royal Armouries

Overall rating: ★ ★ ★

Classification:	Armour	Readability:	★ ★ ★
Updating:	Monthly	Content:	★ ★
Navigation:	★ ★	Speed:	★ ★ ★

UK

This site looks like one for the future. The links work smoothly, the layout and use of images is all of a piece, and there is plenty of information about events, lecture programs, corporate facilities and the like, along with handouts for teachers in a downloadable PDF format. However, there is no information about the actual collections. The Armouries are also responsible for the Tower of London and Fort Nelson, both of which have web pages here. It would be difficult for either to be less high profile, though, and it is fortunate that the guards at the Tower of London have taken it upon themselves to put the Tower of London on the net properly.

The shop has a range of items and books but, unfortunately, they are only available via a printed order form. Still, you can at least email a request for a catalogue. To give a sense of the range, the museum sells scarves, cufflinks, books about fighting and killing and, rather bizarrely, Mother of Pearl inlaid wooden boxes.

Given its recent move from the Tower of London and its lavish redesign, the website is currently rather uninspiring. Still, perhaps it will improve in time.

want to read **more reviews** on this subject?

log on to

www.thegoodwebguide.co.uk

OTHER SITES OF INTEREST

Admiral Nimitz Museum, USA

www.nimitz-museum.org/

If you ignore the rather garish red text, there is a lot of wartime naval photography and ephemera on display here. With the museum itself being based at Pearl Harbour, much of the material is based on the Second World War and the infamous Japanese attack. This is represented by a selection of photographs of the attack and sound recordings of news reports from the period. This military disaster is complemented by accounts of the more serene activities of the Nimitz centre in commemoration of the dead and reconciliation with Japan. You can support these activities if you buy books, posters and collectables from the shop, which offers you an order form to print out and mail/fax.

The Cabinet War Rooms

www.iwm.org.uk/cabinet/index.html

The site contains brief details and images of the various rooms in Churchill's wartime bunker. The feel is rather like that of a pamphlet turned into a website. Shopping is via the Imperial War Museum's website.

HMS Belfast

www.iwm.org.uk/belfast/index.htm

Given that it appears within the Imperial War Museum's site HMS Belfast enjoys a detailed and well-illustrated site. An extensive history of the ship and its antecedents is provided, from its launch just before the Second World War to its decommissioning after the Korean War. There are illustrated accounts of all the major areas of the ship.

Manston Spitfire and Hurricane Memorial, UK

www.spitfire-museum.com/

Dedicated to Britain's wartime Hurricane and Spitfire pilots and machines, this site provides a decent web presence for this museum in Kent. For those unable to get there, the designers describe the history of the collection and the vital role of these fighter planes in the Second World War. There is a community feel here, with reminiscences, remembrance programs and a forum for people to raise any Spitfire-related matters. Where else could you read an Italian request for technical blueprints for a plane over 50 years old!

Museum of Army Transport, UK

www.museum-of-army-transport.co.uk/

Opening with the rather sententious statement that 'all warfare is about the movement of forces', the site goes on to describe the history of the Royal Army Transport Corps from the First World War. Included are examples of army staff cars, trains and tank transporters, mostly illustrated and laid out in a pleasing graphic style. Note that links often only appear if you hover over a image or word long enough.

Museum of British Road Transport, Coventry

www.mrbt.co.uk

For an initially unprepossessing subject the Museum of Road Transport is full of beans, proudly – if not terribly grammatically – lauding 'The Worlds largest display of British Road Transport all under one roof'. Featuring historic lorries, cars and bikes, the museum is probably unchallenged in its boast.

The Museum of the Royal Artillery

www.firepower.org.uk

Being developed at the time of review, this looks like it will be an exciting new museum with a complementary website. They have received a lot of sponsorship and the site is full of pictures of the construction work at the museum. The links section contains useful links to each of the regimental sites.

National Arsenal, Vienna, Austria

www.bmlv.gv.at/hgm/index.html

As small as it is, this site gives a very good sense of a stimulating museum with some unique exhibits; view the jacket worn by Arch Duke Franz Ferdinand when he was shot in Sarajevo in 1914, or the chaise-longue that he died on.

Both of these contrast with a collection that is fecund with tanks, guns and flags, all of which appear on the site. The moral tone is neutral and most of the museum describes events prior to the 1914-18 war, before which the achievements of the Austro-Hungarian empire in creating an army from a massive patchwork of peoples is certainly fascinating. Indeed, if surfers just visited this and Schönbrunn (see p.63) they might think that Austrian history ceased with the end of the Austro-Hungarian empire; which we suppose it did, in a way.

National Museum of Rowing, UK
www.nrm.co.uk
This one is probably somewhat of an acquired taste. Have a look if you're interested in rowing, as it's full of information about the history of the sport, its venues, its events and so on. Where it does less well, however, is in its use of an amateurish blue and yellow font on a white background. This, coupled with the number of unnecessary links (taking you back to the top of a two-paragraph page), can cause irritation after a few minutes.

Stibbert Museum, Florence
www.vps.it/propart/stibbere.htm
Anyone with even a passing interest in military history and/or historical costume should check out this site and, if possible, visit the museum itself in Florence. Like Soane, Stibbert was a 19th-century collector who turned his house into a museum. The site depicts some of the rooms from his palace, allowing browsers to revel in glorious exhibits which include dozens of life-size models wearing the armour and costumes that Stibbert spent his lifetime collecting. These images are surprisingly quick to download and all of them expand to full screen if you double click on them.

Windermere Steam Boat Museum
www.steamboat.co.uk
Make sure you scroll right down to the bottom of the page to find the navigation links. This site describes the facilities at Windermere, and offers an extensive catalogue of books, cassettes, postcards, and assorted memorabilia connected to yachting and sailing. You can also find details of the accommodation that is available here.

have you registered for free updates?

log on to

www.thegoodwebguide.co.uk

virtual museums and web directories

At first glance, the title of this chapter seems like a tautology: after all, everything in this book has a virtual existence. This chapter, though, is devoted to those collections, museums and facilities that only exist on the web. That is not to say that they have no physical existence; only that it is most likely to be just an office somewhere rather than a monumental exhibition space. Typically, these sites act as digests of the collections and exhibitions of the other museums found here. Thus the gallery channel has many of the same images and captions as those found on the museums discussed in Chapter one.

If you are looking for general sites of interest within a specific area, the best bet is probably one of the National Trust or English Heritage sites (see p.109 and 110). The directory sites found in this this chapter would be of use to those who are looking for particularly obscure museums and aren't too fussy about how far they might have to travel to see collections on particular themes.

www.guggenheim.org/exhibitions/virtual/
Virtual Guggenheim

Overall rating: ★ ★ ★ ★			
Classification:	Web museum	**Readability:**	★ ★ ★
Updating:	Monthly	**Content:**	★ ★ ★ ★ ★
Navigation:	★ ★	**Speed:**	★ ★ ★

(US)

Appearing as an option on the homepage for all the Guggenheim foundations, this web page is stylish but a little confusing. The virtual museum is to be finished next year, and is currently a sophisticated series of concept graphics with some dense text. In conjunction with a leading firm of New York architects, this virtual museum will have an architectural structure that exists on the internet rather than having a series of collections floating independently. Promised for the future is a cyber theatre and an information space, which seems to be a sort of digital atrium where surfers can meet and discuss the contents of the digital museum. These are very stimulating as a series of concepts and aspirations, though we wonder whether the final result will live up to the ambition.

SPECIAL FEATURES

Brandon The next offering is a multi-authored account of the life and existence of Brandon Teena, the woman who passed as a man in Falls City, Nebraska in the early 1990s. Entering the site, at your discretion, by clicking on the frenetically morphing design in the centre of the page will bring up an ever-changing collage of images covering themes of sexuality, identity and death; the back button is the only way out. Clicking on the text below the icon allows users to enter the site proper, as it were. Here, through the work of a variety of artists and individuals, the story of his rape and murder is recounted. The responses to his life and death range from collages to poetry and fantasy stories about Brandon and hermaphrodites throughout history. These occasionally bizarre, understandably pretty bleak pieces have some poignant comments to make about sexuality and outsiders in contemporary society. Be aware, though, that some of the images, both actual and imagined, could be disturbing. Generally, this is an innovative approach that may need some more traditional rigour to make any impact. Like the 'mongrel' site developed as part of the Tate Modern's website, the concept of Brandon's story, as told here, is contemporary and sophisticated.

Cyberatlas This represents a valiant attempt to 'map' cyberspace; whether this is possible in any true sense is not an issue that this site seems willing to tackle. Instead, across many incredibly over-designed pages, the designers try to describe cyberspace and the issues involved in mapping it. The results are visually impressive but conceptually bizarre and perhaps even pointless. Important ideas about the nature of knowledge, its dissemination and the role of so-called new media are analysed in the conceptual background to these maps. 'Maps' is something of a misnomer; they appear to be more like a series of disjointed Venn Diagrams. Navigation can be difficult at first in this site, so just remember that the initial screens are actually in two parts. You need to resize your browser window to see either side.

Awe-inspiring in its scope, with some stunning visuals and concepts.

www.nationaltrust.org.uk
The National Trust

Overall rating: ★ ★ ★ ★			
Classification:	Directory	Readability:	★ ★ ★ ★
Updating:	Monthly	Content:	★ ★ ★ ★
Navigation:	★ ★	Speed:	★ ★

UK 🔒

As befits the largest heritage organisation within the UK, the National Trust website should prove appealing for anyone interested in visiting cultural sites within the UK. Due to the breadth of activities and interests that the Trust runs, the site can be a little confusing. The links in the centre of the homepage are as important as those that flash away enticingly on the left-hand side of the screen; those on the left-hand side of the page are untitled so you have to hover the cursor over them in order to find out what each does. In fact, they lead to a series of stimulating pages, including Trusty the Hedgehog's children's area and Tours of the English Coast. This is also the area to look for details of working holidays, conservation and charitable donations and covenants to the benefit of the trust.

There are some QuickTime views of three properties (Corfe Castle, Petworth House, and Durdle Door) here, along with an online bookshop, but the largest area of the site is the guide to the individual properties. The Trust runs 268 sites, so there is plenty to choose from here. The property index is searchable by name, region, or themes. The regional search seems likely to be used the most, enabling people to plan trips to areas within the country. The descriptions of the properties could perhaps give more details about their context and historical significance, but the visitor facilities (cafés, tours, ticket prices and the like) are fully described.

SPECIAL FEATURES

Online Bookshop The online bookshop has a range of about 60 books, available using secure online credit card payment software. The books are divided into those for Kids, Cooking, Gardening, the History of the Houses, and the Trust's range of Handbooks and Guides – that should give you an idea of the choice available. Postage and packing is free within the UK. Online security seems to be satisfactory; the credit card details are encrypted and unique reference numbers are generated for each order. To purchase an item, click on the shopping basket icon next to its name. When you've finished your purchases, click on the icon of the till to pay. We expect that the rest of the National Trust's extensive product range will appear on the site soon. Currently, details of the Trust's wide selection of organic foods can be downloaded in Acrobat format from the section entitled Merchandise and Gifts.

Holiday and Travel Though few details of the Trust's large number of holiday cottages appear here, there is a useful

section detailing the late bookings available at reduced cost. Furthermore, you can request copies of the Trust's glossy holiday brochure. Given the locations and properties that the Trust control, it comes highly recommended.

Grand Turk Tour The highlight of these pages is the Virtual Tour of the Grand Turk ship. Unusually, the designers have chosen to use a program called IPIX rather than the more common QuickTime Player; though the zoom facility is not as good as QuickPlayer's, IPIX generally works more effectively. The images are sharper, though navigation is slightly harder; more importantly there is also sound, so as you stand on the deck you can hear the flapping of the sails in the wind. (Below decks, though, all you can hear is the monotonous drone of the engines.) The IPIX download is quick – about five minutes – and most new machines will have the plug-in already installed. If you follow the link called 'get IPIX', confirming your name and email address, the site will then check your PC for the plug-in. The viewer will start automatically when IPIX has downloaded.

Very lively and informative coverage of the numerous properties and sites cared for by the premier heritage organisation in the UK.

www.english-heritage.org.uk/
English Heritage

Overall rating: ★ ★ ★			
Classification:	Directory	**Readability:**	★ ★ ★ ★
Updating:	Regular	**Content:**	★ ★ ★ ★
Navigation:	★ ★ ★	**Speed:**	★ ★ ★

(GR)

English Heritage is the government organisation responsible for many of Britain's oldest historic sites, Stonehenge and Hadrian's Wall being the most well-known. Some of the major sites have their own websites, of which some are reviewed in this chapter, but for many important sites their web presence is as part of this site. With its use of warm red hues, it has a more coherent feel than the site of its obvious rival, the National Trust. The Days Out section features a similar property search feature to that in the National Trust website; properties can be found by region or thematically.

One oddity is the type of themes chosen by both English Heritage and the National Trust. For example, it is possible to find properties that have ghosts or that have been used in films but not possible to find them by period or style. Still, the English Heritage site does distinguish between different kinds of properties (churches or ruined castle versus country houses) in a way that the National Trust one does not. Descriptions of the properties are often no more than adequate but as a guide for potential visitors the site works very well. Many of the properties run seasonal special events, often with a universal theme for the year. Details for this year can be found in the Discoveries section describing the events on a regional basis.

The shop currently has a large catalogue of guide books, along with books dealing with English history, archaeology,

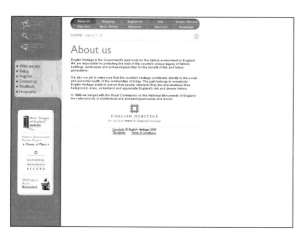

www.thegallerychannel.com
The Gallery Channel

Overall rating: ★ ★ ★			
Classification:	Directory	**Readability:**	★ ★
Updating:	Daily	**Content:**	★ ★ ★ ★
Navigation:	★ ★ ★	**Speed:**	★ ★ ★ ★

UK

and architecture. All of these will soon be purchasable online, according to the site. The gifts catalogue is only available if you email or phone English Heritage. The Kids area contains details of the various education packs and CDs that are available from English Heritage. By way of a sample from their CD-ROMS there is a paper model building of a Roman Villa for children to download, print and then make.

Vivid, wide-ranging and ideal for anyone touring Britain.

The Gallery Channel has a vast amount of reviews, listings and information about museums and galleries worldwide, the main trouble being that there is so much of it. It makes you feel guilty for not being able to go and see that new avant-garde exhibition in that gallery you've never heard of. As a means of broadening definitions of art and art exhibitions the Gallery Channel performs well, although perhaps it does spread too little material of quality over too much analytical bread here. Still, if you need to keep up with gallery news you should bookmark this site and check it most days – it certainly keeps up to date. A lot of the material comes from press releases, though, so you should be aware that much of the analysis is propaganda produced by various museums' press departments.

Updated daily, this site contains a vast amount of information, making it essential surfing for anyone with a serious interest in the UK's museums.

www.historic-scotland.gov.uk/sw-frame.htm		
Historic Scotland		
Overall rating: ★ ★ ★		
Classification: Directory	**Readability:**	★ ★
Updating: Regular	**Content:**	★ ★
Navigation: ★ ★ ★	**Speed:**	★ ★ ★
UK		

From the navy-blue background to the bombastic prose, this site is characterised by its boldness. If it's probably a little too forthright in promoting the quality of its architectural holdings, this Scottish equivalent of the National Trust still has plenty to be bold about. Using a basic search facility, searching by region or by scrutinising the whole list, potential visitors to Scotland can plan trips to such exciting venues as the evocatively named Biggar Gasworks or various parts of Hadrian's Wall. While it is useful to know that these places exist, it is a pity that Historic Scotland doesn't tell us very much about them. Clicking on any of the sites that the search engine has produced pulls up a window containing (with about three exceptions) a number that we assume to be their map-grid reference number. A handful of sites have some description and pictures but could perhaps have slightly more detailed texts, given the importance of some of the locations covered by these sites.

Anyone looking for some off-the-beaten-track attractions in Scotland should definitely catch this site.

http://museums.ncl.ac.uk/archive/		
Museum of Antiquities		
Overall rating: ★ ★ ★		
Classification: Web museum	**Readability:**	★ ★ ★ ★
Updating: Monthly	**Content:**	★ ★ ★ ★
Navigation: ★ ★ ★	**Speed:**	★ ★ ★
FR		

For a site hosted by a provincial university, this virtual museum is startlingly good. The object of the month is genuinely updated monthly, and previous selections can be found in the gallery section. These objects are well-illustrated and described, and many items are photographed from a variety of angles – although this facility is probably wasted on five views of a waterlogged medieval shoe! Scrolling down the homepage, anyone interested in finding out more about Hadrian's Wall should follow links to Walnet. Anyone disappointed by the level of information on the official Hadrian's Wall site should look here to find images of reconstructions, archaeological digs and accounts of life on the wall. This account is supplemented by an Aerial Photography Database containing aerial photographs of a variety of historical sites in the North East, icluding Hadrian's Wall and many medieval villages.

SPECIAL FEATURES

The Armaterium The Armaterium is an encyclopaedia of Roman arms and armour that, despite having a series of FAQs of interest to all, is specifically for experts or at least the seriously interested. None of the samples are illustrated but the site is a compelling resource for bibliographies and accounts of international finds of Roman arms and armour. Anyone wanting to know the Latin for arms catalogue web master should also have a look (it's curator operas).

Virtual Temple of Mithras Though not as slick as some of the QuickPlayer features, this tour works very well. The viewer turns slowly round the room and can click on various statues, reliefs or architectural features. Detailed descriptions and proper photographs then appear, along with an analysis of the objects including a consideration of their purpose within the mythology of Mithras.

A wonderful, if occasionally amateur resource for anyone interested in the classical world.

www.24hourmuseum.org.uk
The 24 Hour Museum

Overall rating: ★ ★ ★			
Classification:	Directory	Readability:	★ ★ ★
Updating:	Weekly	Content:	★ ★ ★
Navigation:	★ ★	Speed:	★ ★ ★

(UK)

Created under the aegis of the UK government department for museums, this busy site has a range of news and reviews of museum sites within the UK. The tone and feel are both resolutely upbeat, with primary colours and a lot of icons on a white background. The primary purpose of the site seems to be to signpost the existence of vast numbers of the most obscure museums in the UK. To this end there are numerous search facilities within the site that will cheerily bring you details of the Museum of Left-Handed Knitting – or some such – and then tell you that it's closed for repairs. You can impose selection criteria on the products of your searches by geography and season but, as with many of the museum websites, you rather have to know what you are looking for before you start searching.

On the more positive side, this site is definitely the one to come to for up-to-date information on new galleries, launches and general museum news from within the UK. That's because, to some extent at least, the information is all 'official' rather than the hearsay that makes up a lot of website content.

Useful central information point for all the UK museums.

www.jinjapan.org/museum/openru.html			
The Virtual Museum of Traditional Japanese Art			
Overall rating: ★ ★ ★			
Classification: Web museum		**Readability:**	★ ★ ★
Updating: Unclear		**Content:**	★ ★ ★
Navigation: ★ ★ ★ ★		**Speed:**	★ ★ ★

UK

Make sure you click on the text saying Virtual Museum (etc) to enter this site, as otherwise your visit will be short lived. It should be made clearer that this is what you have to do; otherwise, you might wait for hours thinking that the computer still had material to download. Once you're in you'll be faced with a sophisticated site map complete with graphics and images denoting what looks like a complex, layered system of navigation. Actually, the navigation and structure are simple, and it is easy to find as much or as little about various Japanese arts as you might wish.

The range of areas defined as 'Traditional Japanese Art' is diffuse. Painting, sculpture, flower arranging, Bonsai, tea ceremonies, sumo wrestling, karate and many others are all described. Karate is included solely on the basis that other people (Westerners) think of it as a traditional Japanese art. The historical background to each art is well explained through expandable pictures and a detailed text. Painting and Ukiyoe are well covered, while the work of different artists and periods is discussed.

A very useful standing point for anyone looking to explore Japanese artistic and cultural mores.

www.4museums.com			
4Museums			
Overall rating: ★ ★			
Classification: Directory		**Readability:**	★ ★ ★
Updating: Unclear		**Content:**	★ ★
Navigation: ★ ★ ★		**Speed:**	★ ★

UK

If you ignore all the adverts and banners that appear, this site has a workable and occasionally useful list of museum and gallery sites on the web. The list itself is rather limited but each site has a short review and the US coverage is competent. International museums are covered rather sparsely and some of the choices are rather bizarre. However, within the US the list of, say, Sports Museums seems to be unique on the web. Though museums dedicated to ice hockey or American football teams may not be to everyone's tastes, this site is definitely performing a useful service in directing people to their websites.

Very good coverage of some of the less well-known museums in the US.

OTHER SITES OF INTEREST

Museums & Galleries – 123 World
www.123world.com/museumsandgalleries/
This is a potentially useful site, providing links to hundreds of museum homepages worldwide. However, it's mainly American sites that are featured and there's no attempt to categorise them, either qualitatively or thematically.

Museumlink's Museum of Museums
www.museumlink.com/internat.htm
Although this site is truly international, its alphabetical list of countries and their museums probably only reaches about 25 per cent of its potential. The list of countries is impressive but the museums featured are fairly haphazardly chosen. Furthermore, the style of the site makes it look amateurish and generates even less confidence than is engendered by some of its rather odd choices.

Museums Around UK on the Web
www.icom.org/vlmp/uk.html
Find your way around online museums and resources relating to museums in the UK here. The website draws your attention to recent additions or particularly impressive sites with either a '!' or a star respectively. You can search them out in alphabetical or geographical order; alternatively, if you only want the cream of the crop, the star sites have been singled out for you. Teeming with links and brief but solidly authoritative information about the websites and museums, it's an efficient, well-organised resource, the usefulness of which supersedes its bland design.

Virtual Library Museums Pages
www.icom.org/vlmp
The same as the above, except international. This is an excellent, eclectic directory of online museums and museum-related resources, and an essential stop-off point for any first exploration of museums on the world wide web. Organised by country and continent, it provides an option to track down your area of choice by key word, and selects recommended virtual museums, major art galleries (although the range for these isn't huge), museums of international significance, museums for children and computer-related museums. There are regular announcements about the museums pages, too, should you find yourself popping back to the portal from time to time.

Cornucopia
www.cornucopia.org.uk
Through a comprehensive database, Cornucopia aims to provide you with a complete picture of all the collections in museums across the UK. It's simple and clear to use, and you can browse by Subject, Geographical Coverage, Collection Location, World Culture and Date/Timeline. Where the website excels is in providing good, detailed information on whatever particular museum you're interested in, letting you know what kind of facilities it offers and rating the size of its collection, how complete the collection is and what its overall strengths are. The picture gallery and news sections weren't exactly rammed to the hilt when we visited – the latter consisted of an announcement that there would be news when they had any, which hardly qualifies as news in itself – but the database is exemplary.

Art Net
www.artnet.com
A comprehensive, illustrated listing of international galleries, exhibitions, auctions and the works of over 16 000 artists.

ICA New Media Centre
www.newmediacentre.com
A new initiative from the ICA dedicated to digital art. The site includes screensavers and online digital art projects.

Escape for a day

There's nothing quite like a change of scenery to revive your spirits, is there? To unwind and relax and enjoy time spent with your family and friends.

If you're in need of a little escapism, then the National Trust can offer you endless changes of scenery. From magical mediaeval castles to stately moated manor houses. Lose yourself in acres of unspoilt parkland or one of our magnificent gardens. Or, take part in one of our many special events.

Why not let yourself go this weekend? We are open throughout the Summer till the end of Autumn.

Call us on 0870 458 4000 or visit www.nationaltrust.org.uk to find out more about escaping to a National Trust property near you.

Call 0870 458 4000 or visit www.nationaltrust.org.uk

 THE NATIONAL TRUST

Glossary of Internet Terms

Accelerators Add-on programs, which speed up browsing.

Acceptable Use Policy Terms and conditions of using the internet, usually set by organisations who wish to regulate an individual's use of the internet. For example, an employer might issue a ruling on the type of email which can be sent from an office.

Access Provider A company which provides access to the internet, usually via a dial-up account. Companies such as AOL and Dircon charge for this, although there are an increasing number of free services such as Freeserve, Lineone and Tesco.net. Also known as an Internet Service Provider.

Account A user's internet connection, with an Access/Internet Service Provider which usually has to be paid for.

Acrobat Reader Small freely-available program, or web browser plug-in, which lets you view a Portable Document Format (PDF) file.

Across Lite Plug-in which allows you to complete crossword puzzles online.

Address Location name for an email or internet site, which is the online equivalent of a postal address. It is usually composed of a unique series of words and punctuation, such as *my.name@house.co.uk*. See also URL.

America Online (AOL) World's most heavily subscribed online service provider.

Animated GIF Low-grade animation technique which is used on websites.

ASCII Stands for American Standard Code for Information Interchange. It is a coding standard which all computers can recognise, ensuring that if a character is entered on one part of the internet, the same character will be seen elsewhere.

ASCII Art Art made of letters and other symbols. Made up of simple text, so it can be recognised by different computers.

ASDL Stands for Asynchronous Digital Subscriber Line, which is a high speed copper wire which will allow rapid transfer of information. Not widely in use at moment, though the government is pushing for its early introduction.

Attachment A file included with an email, which may be composed of text, graphics and sound. Attachments are encoded for transfer across the internet, and can be viewed in their original form by the recipient. An attachment is the equivalent of putting a photograph with a letter in the post.

Bookmark A function of the Netscape Navigator browser which allows you to save a link to your favourite sites, so that you can return straight there without re-entering the address. Favourites in Internet Explorer is the same thing.

BPS Abbreviation of Bits Per Second, which is a measure of the speed at which information is transferred or downloaded.

Broadband A type of data transfer medium (usually a cable or wire) which can carry several signals at the same time. Most existing data transfer media are narrowband, and can only carry one signal at a time.

Browse Common term for looking around the web. See also Surfing.

Browser A generic term for the software that allows users to move and look around the Web. Netscape Navigator and Internet Explorer are the ones that most people are familiar with, accounting for 97 per cent of web hits.

Bulletin Board Service A BBS is a computer with a telephone connection, which allows you direct contact to upload and download information and converse with other users, via the computer. It was the forerunner to the online services and virtual communities of today.

Cache A temporary storage space on the hard drive of your computer, which stores downloaded websites. When you return to a website, information is retrieved from the cache and displayed more rapidly. This information may not be the most recent version for sites which are frequently updated; you will need to reload the website address for these.

Chat Talking to other users on the web in real time, but with typed instead of spoken words. Special software such as ICQ or MIRC is required before you can chat.

Chat Room An internet channel which allows several people to type in their messages and talk to one another over the internet.

Clickstream The trail that you leave as you 'click' your way around the web.

Codec Any technology which can compress/decompress data, such as MPEG and MP3.

Content The material on a website that actually relates to the site, and is hopefully of interest or value. Things like adverts are not considered to be part of the content. The term is also used to refer to information on the internet that can be seen by users, as opposed to programming and other background information.

Cookie A cookie is a nugget of information sometimes sent by websites to your hard drive when you visit. They contain such details as what you looked at, what you ordered, and can add more information, so that the website can be customised to suit you.

Cybercafe Cafe where you can use a computer terminal to browse the net for a small fee.

Cyberspace When first coined by the sci-fi author William Gibson, it meant a shared hallucination which occured when people logged on to computer networks. Now, it refers to the virtual space you're in when on the internet.

Dial Up A temporary telephone connection to your ISP's computer and how you make contact with your ISP, each time you log onto the Internet.

Domain The part of an Internet address which identifies an individual computer, and can often be a business or person's name. For example, in the goodwebguide.com the domain name is theGoodWebGuide.

Download Transfer of information from an Internet server to your computer.

Dynamic HTML Most recent version of the HTML standard.

Ecash Electronic cash, used to make transactions on the internet.

Ecommerce The name for business which is carried out over the internet.

Email Mail delivered electronically over the internet. Usually comprised of text messages, but can contain illustrations, music and animations. Mail is sent to an email address: the internet equivalent of a postal address.

Encryption A process whereby information is scrambled to produce a 'coded message', so that it can't be read while in transit on the internet. The recipient must have decryption software in order to read the message.

Expire Term referring to newsgroup postings which are automatically deleted after a fixed period of time.

Ezine Publication on the web, which is updated regularly.

FAQ Stands for frequently asked questions and is a common section on websites where the most common enquiries and their answers are archived.

Frame A method which splits web pages into several windows.

FTP/File Transfer Protocol Standard method for transporting files across the internet.

GIF/Graphics Interchange Format A format in which graphics are compressed, and a popular method of putting images onto the internet, as they take little time to download.

Gopher Precursor of the world wide web, consisting of archives accessed via a menu and organised by subject.

GUI/Graphical User Interface. This is the system which turns binary information into the words and images format you can see on your computer screen. For example, instead of seeing the computer language which denotes the presence of your toolbar, you actually see a toolbar.

Hackers A term used to refer to expert programmers who use their skills to break into computer systems, just for the fun of it. Nowadays the word is more commonly associated with computer criminals, or Crackers.

Header Basic indication of what's in an email: who it's from, when it was sent, and what it's about.

Hit When a file is downloaded from a website it is referred to as a 'hit'. Measuring the number of hits is a rough method of counting how many people visit a website. Not wholly accurate as one website can contain many files, so one visit may generate several hits.

Homepage Usually associated with a personal site, but also refers to the first page on your browser, or the first page of a website.

Host Computer on which a website is stored. A host computer may store several websites, and usually has a fast, powerful connection to the internet. Also known as a Server.

HTML/Hypertext Mark-Up Language The computer code used to construct web pages.

HTTP/Hypertext Transfer Protocol The protocol for moving HTML files across the web.

Hyperlink A word or graphic formatted so that when you click on it, you move from one area to another. See also hypertext.

Hypertext Text within a document, formatted so it acts as a link between pages, or from one document to another.

Image Map A graphic which contains hyperlinks.

Interface What you actually see on the computer screen.

Internet One or more computers connected to one another is an internet (lower case i). The Internet is the biggest of all the internets, consisting of a worldwide collection of interconnected computer networks.

Internet Explorer One of the most popular pieces of browser software, produced by Microsoft.

Intranet A network of computers which works in the same way as an internet but for internal use, such as within a corporation.

ISDN/Integrated Services Digital Network Digital telephone line which facilitates fast connections, transfers large amounts of data and can carry more than one form of data.

ISP/Internet Service Provider See Access Provider.

Java Programming language which can be used to create interactive multimedia effects on web pages. Used to create programmes known as *applets* that add features such as animations, sound and even games to websites.

Javascript A scripting language which, like Java, can be used to add extra multimedia features. However, it does not consist of separate programmes. Javascript is embedded into the HTML text and can interpreted by the browser, provided that the user has a javascript enabled browser.

JPEG Stands for 'Joint Photographic Experts Group' and is the name given to a type of format which compresses photos so that they can be seen on the web.

Kill file A function which allows a user to block incoming information from unwanted sources. Normally used on email and newsreaders.

LAN/Local Area Network A type of internet, but limited to a single area, such as an office.

Login The account name or password needed to access a computer system.

Link Connection between web pages, or between one web document and another, which are accessed via formatted text and graphic.

Mailing List A discussion group which is associated with a website. Participants send their emails to the site, and it is copied and sent by the server to other individuals on the mailing list.

Modem A device for converting digital data into analogue signals for transmission along standard phone lines. The usual way for home users to connect to the internet or log into their email accounts. May be internal (built into the computer) or external (a desk-top box connected to the computer).

MP3 A compressed music file format, which has almost no loss of quality although the compression rate may be very high.

Netiquette Guidelines for polite behaviour when exchanging information with people on the net.

Netscape Popular browser, now owned by AOL.

Newbie Term for someone new to the Internet. Used pejoratively of newcomers to bulletin boards or chat, who commit the sin of asking obvious questions or failing to observe the 'netiquette'.

Newsgroup Discussion group made up of Internet users who share an interest. There are thousands of newsgroups covering every possible subject.

Offline Not connected to the internet, therefore saving telephone charges if you connect through a telephone line.

Online Connected to the internet.

Offline Browsing A function of the browser software, which allows the user to download pages and read them while they are offline.

Online Service Provider Similar to an access provider, but provides additional features such as live chat.

PDF/Portable Document Format A file format created by Adobe for offline reading of brochures, reports and other documents with complex graphic design. Can be read by anyone with Acrobat Reader.

Plug-in Piece of software which adds more functions (such as playing music or video) to another, larger software program.

POP3/Post Office Protocol An email protocol that allows you to pick up your mail from any location on the web.

Portal A website which offers many services, such as search engines, email and chat rooms, and to which people are likely to return to often. ISPs such as Yahoo and Alta Vista provide portal sites which are the first thing you see when you log on, and in theory act as gateways to the rest of the web.

Post/Posting Information sent to a usenet group, bulletin board, message board or by email.

PPP/Point to Point Protocol The agreed way of sending data over dial-up connections, so that the user's computer, the modem and the Internet Server can all recognise it. It is the protocol which allows you to get online.

Protocol Convention detailing a set of actions that computers in a network must follow so that they can understand one another.

Query Request for specific information from a database.

RAM /Random Access Memory Your computer's short-term memory.

Realplayer A plug-in program that allows you to view video in real-time and listen to sound and which is becoming increasingly important for web use.

Router An interface between two networks that decides how to route information.

Searchable Database A database on a website which allows the user to search for information, usually be keyword.

Search Engine Programs which enable web users to search for pages and sites using keywords. They are usually to be found on portal sites and browser homepages. Infoseek, Alta Vista and Lycos are some of the popular search engines.

Secure Transactions Information transfers which are encrypted so that only the sender and recipient have access to the uncoded message, so that the details within remain private. The term is most commonly used to refer to credit card transactions, although other information can be sent in a secure form.

Server A powerful computer that has a permanent fast connection to the internet. Such computers are usually owned by companies and act as host computers for websites.

Sign-on To connect to the internet and start using one of its facilities.

Shareware Software that doesn't have to be paid for or test version of software that the user can access for free, as a trial before buying it.

Skins Simple software that allows the user to change the appearance of an application.

Standard A style which the whole of the computer industry has agreed upon. Industry standards mean that hardware and software produced by the various different computer companies will work with one another.

Stream A technique for processing data, which enables it to be downloaded as a continuous stream, and viewed or listened to as the data arrives.

Surfing Slang for looking around the Internet, without any particular aim, following links from site to site.

TLA/Three Letter Acronyms Netspeak for the abbreviations of net jargon, such as BPS (Bits Per Second) and ISP (Internet Service Provider).

Upload To send files from your computer to another on the internet. When you send an email you are uploading a file.

URL/Uniform Resource Locator Jargon for an address on the internet, such as www.thegoodwebguide.co.uk.

Usenet A network of newsgroups, which form a worldwide system, on which anyone can post 'news'.

Virtual Community Name given to a congregation of regular mailing list/ newsgroup users.

VRML/Virtual Reality Modeling Language Method for creating 3D environments on the web.

Wallpaper Description of the sometimes hectic background patterns which appear behind the text on some websites.

Web Based Email/Webmail Email accounts such as Hotmail and Rocketmail, which are accessed via an Internet browser rather than an email program such as Outlook Express. Webmail has to be typed while the user is online, but can accessed from anywhere on the Web.

Webmaster A person responsible for a web server. May also be known as System Administrator.

Web Page Document that forms one part of a website (though some sites are a single page), usually formatted in HTML.

Web Ring Loose association of websites which are usually dedicated to the same subject and often contain links to one another.

Website A collection of related web pages which often belong to an individual or organisation and are about the same subject.

World Wide Web The part of the Internet which is easy to get around and see. The term is often mistakely interchanged with Internet, though the two are not the same. If the Internet is a shopping mall, with shops, depots, and delivery bays, then the web is the actual shops which the customers see and use.

Index

The Good Web Guide

www.thegoodwebguide.co.uk

The Good Web Guide provides simple one-click access to all the sites mentioned in this book, and is an easy way to start exploring the internet. All books about the internet become slightly out of date as soon they're printed, but with the free updates you'll receive as a subscriber to the Good Web Guide website, this book will remain current as long as you're a member.

The goodwebguide.co.uk homepage provides links to each of the GWG subject channels, including Museums and Galleries. It also lists headlines and links to some of the newest articles, reviews and competitions on the site, and details of special offers on other Good Web Guide books. Although some reviews and articles are free to view, the majority of the content on the Good Web Guide site is accessible only to members. Begin by clicking on the small 'Register Now' icon near the top left of the page. When you've filled in and submitted your details a menu will appear on the left of the page. Choose the option Register a Purchase. A list of questions will appear, but you only need to answer the one relevant to this book, and you will need to have the book in front of you to find the answer. Once you're registered you'll be able to view the contents of this book online, and be eligible for free updates. As a member you can upgrade to obtain access to all the channels at a specially discounted rate.

Reviews are organised by chapter, with the new reviews in the Latest Additions section. At the bottom of each review there is a link straight to the site, so you don't have to worry about typing in the addresses. New reviews are added at least monthly, sometimes weekly. You can also sign up for monthly free newsletters to have website reviews delivered straight to your desk.

other great titles in thegoodwebguide series:

hardback £12.99

antiques and collectables .... ISBN 1-903282-21-7
genealogy.......................... ISBN 1-903282-06-3
health................................ ISBN 1-903282-08-x
home and interiors .... ISBN 1-903282-15-2
money............................... ISBN 1-903282-26-8
museums and galleries....... ISBN 1-903282-14-4
travel................................ ISBN 1-903282-05-5
wine................................. ISBN 1-903282-04-7
world religions................... ISBN 1-903282-25-x

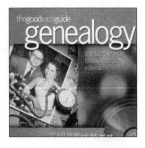

paperback £7.99

food.................................. ISBN 1-903282-17-9
gardening.......................... ISBN 1-903282-16-0
parents............................. ISBN 1-903282-19-5

small paperbacks £4.99

comedy............................. ISBN 1-903282-20-9
games............................... ISBN 1-903282-10-1
gay life............................. ISBN 1-903282-13-6
music............................... ISBN 1-903282-11-x
sex................................... ISBN 1-903282-09-8
sport................................ ISBN 1-903282-07-1
tv..................................... ISBN 1-903282-12-8